Teaching Languages

for Communication and Accuracy

Raymond C. Clark

Janie L. Duncan

Illustrations by Patrick R. Moran

PRO LINGUA ASSOCIATES

Pro Lingua Associates, Publishers
P.O. Box 1348
Brattleboro, Vermont 05302 USA
Office: 802-257-7779
Orders: 800-366- 4775
Email: info@ProLinguaAssociates.com
WebStore www.ProLinguaAssociates.com
SAN: 216-0579

At ***Pro Lingua***
our objective is to foster an approach
to learning and teaching that we call
interplay, *the **inter**action of language*
learners and teachers with their materials,
with the language and culture,
and with each other in active, creative,
*and productive **play**.*

ISBN 13: 978-0-86647-351-4; 10: 0-86647-351-3

This book was designed by A.A. Burrows in collaboration with Ray Clark and Pat Moran. It was set in Arno Pro with sample materials set in Myriad Pro for contrast. Arno Pro is a contemporary type face designed by Robert Simbach for Adobe. He drew inspiration from the classic, humanistic typefaces of Renaissance Italy, type that was used by printers along the Arno River in Florence. The faces are easy to read and yet graceful and calligraphic. It is used in this book both for text and display. The contrasting face used for sample materials is Myriad Pro, an elegant, humanistic san-serif, legible and inviting as text and strong in display. It, too, was developed by Adobe's Robert Simbach with Carol Twombly. The book was printed and bound by Gasch Printing in Odenton, Maryland.

Printed in the United States
Third Edition, first printing 2013. 11,200 copies in print

Contents

Preface

The first edition of this book, originally published in 1980 as *Language Teaching Techniques*, was Pro Lingua's first book, and it helped launch our company as an independent alternative for the language teacher looking for innovation and excitement in their teaching.

When the sales of *Language Teaching Techniques* dropped off in the late nineties, perhaps because so many of our teaching friends owned the book, we let the second edition go out of print. However, teachers kept asking for it, and we kept looking for new ideas, and kept our "LTT" on the list of old projects to bring back to life. About two years ago, Janie Duncan took charge and began revising the techniques and tactics. And so here we are again. Our first "baby," reborn.

This third edition, retitled *Teaching Languages for Communication and Accuracy*, contains much that was in the 1980 edition and much that is new. Needless to say, good, practical teaching practices withstand the pressures of time while new insights into the language teaching-learning situation generate new practices.

On Third Person Pronouns

In this book, Pro Lingua Associates is offering our solution to the vexing *he/she* problem. We have come to the conclusion that when a third person singular pronoun is needed, and that person is indefinite (and hence gender is unknown or unimportant), we will use the third person plural forms *they, them, their, theirs.* We are aware that historically these forms represent grammatical plurality (although the use of *they* as a singular pronoun goes back to Chaucer). However, there are clear instances in the English language where the third person plural form is used to refer to a preceding indefinite, grammatically singular pronoun. Examples:

> *Everyone says this, don't they.*
> *Nobody agrees with us, but we will ignore them.*

If you will accept the examples, it is not a major step to finding the following acceptable:

> *The user of this book should find this easier because they can avoid the confusion and awkwardness of "he" or "she" or "he/she" and the implicit sexism of using "he" for everybody.*

Long ago, English dispensed with *thee, thou, thy, thine* and seems to be functioning quite well with two "yous." So why not two "theys"?

Introduction

Techniques and Tactics: A Definition

We have divided our collection into **techniques** and **tactics**, although both types could easily be labeled teaching practices. Both types are physically observable activity in the language classroom, as opposed to the curricular or methodological organization that governs the day-to-day sequence of classroom activities. Simplistically put, a **technique** has a beginning, middle, and end, not unlike the classical lesson plan format of present, practice, and produce aimed at helping the student achieve communicative competence and **fluency**. On the other hand, a **tactic** is a brief activity that may often be spontaneous and may be as simple as focusing on a troublesome pronunciation pair, or a verb tense construction, or an unplanned vocabulary exploration aimed at improving **accuracy** in listening, pronunciation, word usage, and grammar. The ultimate goal of these practices is a second language speaker who is both fluent and accurate.

Skill Development

The teaching practices in this book should be viewed first and foremost as activities for improving the student's command of the spoken language. Therefore, fluent and accurate speaking skills and successful listening comprehension are the principal objectives of these practices. However, it should be pointed out that many, if not all, of these practices could and probably should be accompanied by activities that also require the students to use the written language. In fact, appropriate reading and writing activities are often suggested within the description of the practice.

Techniques and Tactics Format

The format in which these various practices are presented is rather self-explanatory. The basic information (**Purpose**, **Brief Description**, and **Sample Text**) is presented on the first page. The middle pages contain an **illustration** and the **procedure**. Inexperienced teachers will probably spend most of their time with this essential information. The next two sections (**Variations** and **Suggestions and Guidelines for Developing Your Own Material**) will be of interest to the experienced teacher who may already be familiar with the basic procedures.

We suggest you think of this collection of teaching practices as a collection of basic tools, somewhat analogous to a carpenter's toolbox. Each tool is useful for a specific purpose, but just as a house cannot be built with a hammer alone, neither can a good language program be fashioned from an over-reliance on any one technique or an indiscriminate use of these teaching practices.

Teacher Training

In addition to being a resource for the individual teacher, the teaching practices in this book can serve as a basic teacher training text. It can be used one-on-one for training volunteers, for example, or as part of the curriculum of a teacher training program. The most effective way of using the text would be for the trainer to demonstrate a technique or tactic. (Sometimes this can be done in a language that the trainees do not know.) This could be followed by a discussion of the experience, and then the trainees read at least the first three pages. Finally, each trainee develops a lesson plan using the material in the book or creates a plan and then peer teaches it. Finally the trainee's performance is critiqued. In short:

◆ Trainer Demonstrates

◆ Trainer and Trainees Discuss

◆ Trainees Read

◆ Trainees Plan

◆ Trainees Peer Teach

◆ Trainer and Trainees Critique

Teaching Languages

As indicated in the title, this text can be used, with some adaptation, by teachers of virtually any language. In fact, the original book was based on a teacher training manual developed for the Peace Corps for training teachers of uncommonly taught languages. Obviously, the text and examples are in English so that the content is available to any language teacher who can read English. It is also obvious that some of the practices, especially the pronunciation tactics, will not easily work with other languages. Nevertheless, most of the practices are very adaptable.

Working with Students with LDs

The techniques and tactics in this book employ a variety of modalities – audio, visual (pictorial and alphabetic), and physical, all of which are key to helping all learners access the language, process it, and express themselves. This variety of activities benefits everyone, but it can also can be key to a positive language learning experience for students with learning disabilities, attention deficit disorders with or without hyperactivity (ADHD), and/or autism spectrum disorder (ASD) (referred to here as LDs or students with LD).

Because students with LDs differ in how they take in, manipulate, and produce language, there is not one guaranteed teaching practice. What may help most is to keep in mind how to involve LD students in discovering, exploring, developing, and articulating what works for them. Seek and act on feedback, incorporating what works and discarding what doesn't. The following suggestions on working with LDs are from a variety of websites:

- ◆ Establish routines and a clear agenda
- ◆ Provide explicit explanations
- ◆ Give graphic organizers
- ◆ Provide classwork exploring creative ways of organizing and understanding how the language works
- ◆ Simplify or chunk complex transformations into smaller steps

- ◆ Be patient, allowing students time to formulate responses
- ◆ Offer multi-sensory instruction (kinesthetic, auditory, and visual)
- ◆ Reduce the quantity of material
- ◆ Provide charts of affixes for vocabulary acquisition
- ◆ Do handouts on pastel paper to reduce the sharp contrast of black text on white
- ◆ Be flexible in assessment
- ◆ Recognize and respect the differences and strengths of all learners

Useful Websites on Learning Disabilities

A Guide to Learning Disabilities for the ESL Classroom Practitioner by Christine Root

http://www.cc.kyoto-su.ac.jp/information/tesl-ej/ej01/a.4.html

International Dyslexia Association http://www.interdys.org/index.htm

National Center for Learning Disabilities http://www.ncld.org

Teaching Languages

for

Communication and Accuracy

Rhythmic Rhyme

Purpose

To practice the suprasegmentals of pronunciation (stress, intonation, linking, rhythm) and common lexical items in a catchy poetic chant. Students are not asked to memorize the rhyme, but through repeated practice they can improve their speaking.

Brief Description

A Rhythmic Rhyme is a rhymed chant that may be a list of actions, a dialogue, or a monologue read, practiced, and performed by the whole class, groups, and/or individuals. The chant should be engaging and fun and may be used as a transition activity, before or at the end of class.

Sample Paired Rhythmic Rhymes

Where's your hat?

(Mother)	(Child)
Where's your hat?	On my head.
Where're your gloves?	In my pockets.
Do you have a scarf?	Yeah, right here.
Do you have boots?	On my feet!
A mother's work is never done, never done!	It's OK, Mom. I am 21!

****

Anything for You

Have you got a quarter?	Not for you!
Can you spare a dime?	Maybe one or two.
Do you have a minute?	Maybe I do.
Do you have the time?	Anything for you.

****

Eating Out

Do you have a table? a table for two?	A table by the water?
Yes, that will do.	
Do you have a table? a table for four?	A table in the corner?
A table in the back?	A table by the pool?
Yeah, that's cool.	

Procedure

1. Read the rhyme aloud while the students listen and follow the text on the board, with a handout, or on a projection screen.

2. As you read, the students should mark or note words and phrases they don't understand or know how to pronounce. Then they can ask questions. If they don't, you ask.

3. Define and practice pronouncing new words.

4. Read the chant again and have the students read along with you or just after you. Emphasize the stress and intonation.

5. Start each line with the students; then change to a whisper as they finish the line.

6. Have the students practice and then perform in small groups and/or individually in front of the class.

Variations

1. Read and record the rhyme in the language lab or on computer files. Have the students use the recording for practice in or outside class.

2. Some rhymes (like those in the samples) lend themselves to breaking the class into groups so that one group reads a line and the other group responds to it, etc.

3. Say the lines as syllables: da DA da DA da DA da DA da da DA(A mother's work is never done, never done.) and have the students mimic you and/or say the words.

4. Tap or clap the rhythm as you say the lines.

Suggestions and Guidelines for Writing a Rhythmic Rhyme

1. Use phrases, rituals or words that are immediately useful to students in everyday situations.

2. Keep the phrases short and snappy.

3. Use repetitive lines to focus on the features of the language being practiced.

4. Limericks can also be a good source for short choral readings.

5. Invite the students to form pairs or groups and create a Rhythmic Rhyme.

Note

1. Carolyn Graham's *Jazz Chants* (Oxford University Press) is a well-known source of chants.

2. Pro Lingua's *Rhymes 'n Rhythms* is a collection of relatively easy rhymes.

3. Limericks are featured in *Pronunciation Activities* (Pro Lingua). Each limerick-based lesson is focused on a single vowel sound.

Ritual

Purpose

To have the students memorize set phrases, sentences, or sequences of sentences because (1) the lines are highly predictable and therefore useful in general conversation or (2) the lines contain idiomatic expressions or other "frozen" pieces of language such as greetings, or (3) the lines contain useful examples of a particular grammatical construction and can therefore serve as model sentences for future reference.

Brief Description

A ritual is a very brief conversation. Usually it centers around a common everyday activity involving two people. Because it is intended to be a memorization activity, typically the ritual is composed of short sentences in a very limited number of exchanges. The longer the ritual is, the more unwieldy it becomes for memorization purposes.

Samples

X: Paper or plastic?
Y: Paper, please.
X: Credit or debit?
Y: _____.

S: Excuse me teacher. What does _____ mean?
T: It means _____.
S: Thanks a lot.
T: Don't mention it.

S: Pardon me, teacher. How do you spell _____?
T: It's ___ ___ ___ ___ ___.
S: So, it's ___ ___ ___ ___ ___.
T: Right!/No, it's ___ ___ ___ ___ ___.

Y: I'm sorry, I didn't understand. Could you say that again?
X: Sure, I said, _____.
Y: Thanks.
X: No problem.

Y: Would you mind speaking a bit slower. I'm learning English,
      but I still don't understand everything.
X: Of course. I said _____.
Y: Uhm. I'm sorry. Did you say _____?
X: Yes, that's what I said.

Procedure

1. Present the ritual while the students listen. Repeat it two or three times using gestures, pictures, puppets, etc., to help convey the identity of each speaker and the meaning of the ritual.

2. Ask the students questions about the ritual. This is to make sure that they understand the general sense of the ritual as well as the meaning of individual words.

3. Have the students read the ritual and allow them to ask questions.

4. You say a line and the students repeat the same line. Do this several times for each line until you have practiced repeating the entire ritual.

5. You take part A and the students take part B. You say the first line and the students respond with the second line. This is done for each pair of lines until they can respond easily.

6. Reverse the parts. The students initiate the ritual with Part A and you respond.

7. Have the students practice the ritual in pairs. Move around the room listening and correcting.

8. Have pairs of students perform the ritual to the rest of the class.

Variations

1. Instead of having the students read the ritual in the book, write it on the board. As you repeat and practice the ritual, erase it word by word until nothing remains.

2. In Step 4 (repetitions), vary the repetitions from individual responses to choral responses.

3. Instead of having the students see the written version of the ritual in step 3 (read), have them try to write it out before they have seen the written version. One student can go to the board and write the sentences while the other students contribute the lines, spelling them as best they can. You would correct the students' spelling as you go along.

4. When you have finished all eight steps, give the ritual as a dictation. You read a line and the students write it down. Check their work. Re-creating a written version of the ritual can be a useful "test" of whether the students have learned the ritual well.

5. Have the students re-tell the ritual as a narrative. For example, the re-telling might begin: "The student asked the teacher for the meaning of a word." etc.

6. Use stick figures to cue the students on the sequence of the ritual. The following sequence represents a sample ritual. Note the key:

+ = an affirmative statement   ? = a question
– = a negative statement   ! = an imperative or exclamation

Can I smoke here? Sorry, no smoking here.   Oh, I didn't know. Don't worry about it!

Suggestions and Guidelines for Writing a Ritual

1. Keep the sentences short – on average, fewer than 10 words per line – and keep the ritual short: 4 – 10 lines.

2. Keep the conversation natural and colloquial. Do your lines reflect what people actually say in the given situation? Rituals can be a good place to introduce idioms.

3. Some additional situations that can be cast in a ritualistic format:

◆ greetings and leave-takings
   Hello, how are you?…

◆ brief conversational rituals
   Nice day, isn't it?…

◆ street directions
   Excuse me, where is . . . ?

◆ introductions of people
   John, this is ...

◆ simple inquiries for information
   Excuse me, can you tell me…

◆ buying/bargaining for something
   How much is that…

◆ getting change
   Sorry to bother you.
   Do you have change
   for a _____ ?

◆ asking for help
   Can you help me please?

Note

This technique was devised by Alexander Lipson, a teacher of Russian at Harvard University.

Dialogue

Purpose

To introduce selected aspects of discourse in a colloquial context, with special attention to usage: what people actually say in selected situations. Secondly, to have students acquire these aspects for future use.

Brief Description

A brief conversational exchange is presented and practiced and finally performed orally with minimal resort to the printed version.

Samples

At the Airport Tourist and Information Desk. Tourist and Attendant. (EASY)

T: Excuse me, where can I get a taxi?

A: Go to exit three oh two.

T: Uhm, where's exit three oh two?

A: Down the stairs.

T: Hmm. Where are the stairs?

A: Right there! Through that door!

T: Oh, I see. Thanks.

A: Don't mention it.

Husband and wife talking at home. (HARDER)

Jill: I thought you gave up on bottled water.

Jack: Who said?

Jill: You did. Last week.

Jack: Oh, that was then, and this is now.

Jill: So, you changed your mind?

Jack: Yeah, I guess I did. Bottled water tastes so much better.

Jill: Here, drink this. It's straight from the fridge.

Jack: Hmm, not bad, not bad at all.

Jill: Is it tap or bottled?

Jack: I'm not sure.

Jill: See! You can't tell, can you?

Procedure

1. Set the scene, explaining what is going to happen.

2. Give the students the printed dialogue and read it through once as they listen.

3. Solicit questions. The students may ask about the meaning of the words or grammatical structures.

4. Have the students repeat the lines as a chorus after you.

5. Split the class in half and assign one role to half the class and the other to the other half. Then have the students repeat their parts after you. Again, have the students repeat their parts after you, but this time initiate each line with just the first two or three words.

6. Pair up the students and have them practice together.

7. Ask for volunteers to "perform" the dialogue with you as the prompter.

Variations

There are many possible variations on the procedure previously outlined. A few are:

1. Instead of giving the students the script, divide the board in half. Say a line and then write the first word for each line on the board, for example:

Tourist	Attendant
Excuse me, . . .	*Go to . . .*
Uhm, where's . . .	*Down . . .*
etc.	

   Then continue as above. Finally, erase all but the first letter in each line.

2. After working with the dialogue, have pairs write a similar dialogue with one person asking *"where"* questions. As they finish, check their dialogues for accuracy. Then ask for volunteers to perform the dialogues.

3. After step 4, above, you say one part, and the students respond in chorus with the second part. First, you start the dialogue as T and they respond as A; then they start the dialogue as T and you respond with A.

4. The dialogue can be used as a writing exercise, especially for working on direct and/or reported speech.

Suggestions and Guidelines for Writing a Dialogue

1. For best results, with lower proficiency students confine the dialogue to six lines and not more than eight words per line.

2. Dialogues can be a useful vehicle for introducing discourse markers such as *hmm, oh, really, so.* They can also be useful for illustrating first and subsequent article usage (a > the).

3. Dialogues illustrating modal verbs can be useful, as modals are often better introduced and practiced in a meaningful context.

Notes

1. For several years dialogues were a very common format for presenting second language material. Too often, students were asked to memorize an entire dialogue which they would never have the chance to use. However, dialogues can still serve a useful purpose, as outlined in this technique.

2. Certain comic strips can be a useful source of dialogues. Check out *Peanuts, Doonesbury,* and *Sally Forth.*

Spiel

Purpose

To use a short, spontaneous monologue that will serve as the basis for listening and speaking practice. A secondary purpose is to introduce the students to new vocabulary and grammatical constructions, and a final purpose is to give the students practice in learning how to learn from a monologue.

Brief Description

This technique does not necessarily use written material; it is spoken and it is created in the classroom. Therefore, it resembles real speech more than a formal speech does, because it is produced spontaneously. There are several ways that a spiel can be used in the classroom, but the basic procedure is for the students to be able to comprehend and, after practice, to either reproduce the spiel or create their own version of the spiel.

Sample Word List for a Spiel

A 30-second talk about your family.		
mother	grandfather	cousin
father	grandmother	living/alive
sister	uncle	dead
brother	aunt	married
single		

Procedure

1. Plan your spiel by deciding on a topic and then creating a word list as the basis for your spiel.

2. Give the spiel. Have one of the learners act as the timekeeper. They will stop you after 30 seconds. It is very important to stop, even though you may not say everything you want to. Talk at normal speed. Don't make it into a speech; keep it informal.

3. Repeat the spiel. It is all right to change it slightly, but do not make it longer or add new material. It is no longer necessary to be timed, so you can slow down your speech somewhat as long as you don't add new material.

4. Allow the students to ask questions about the material. It may be useful to put some of the new words on the board.

5. Say the spiel a final time at normal speed.

6. Ask the students questions about the material.

7. Ask a volunteer to give the spiel. If the spiel is difficult, pair or group the learners. This makes the spiel a group effort with everybody contributing what they know. Finally, ask individuals to give the spiel as accurately as they can to each other.

Variations

1. A spiel could be based on a picture, with or without an accompanying word list.

2. To help the students recall the sequence of sentences in the spiel, put a key word from each sentence on the board.

3. As a final step you can have the students write out the spiel.

4. Bring in a friend to give a spiel on some topic that they are familiar with.

5. Write out the spiel before class and read it aloud. This allows for repetitions to be consistent.

6. Use a voice recorder either to prepare a spiel or to record one in class.

Suggestions and Guidelines for Developing a Spiel

1. Ask the students to suggest spiel topics to you.

2. Spiels can be quite useful for building new vocabulary, but try to limit the new words. Adjust the length of the sentences to the level of the class. At the same time, try to keep the spiel as natural as possible.

3. Although the 30 second rule is somewhat flexible, it will usually produce a spiel of about 75 words, a reasonable piece of language for a class to work on.

4. Choose topics that are not too abstract. Some suggestions are:
   - ◆ My family
   - ◆ An occupation, trade, or profession
   - ◆ A national holiday
   - ◆ A game or sport
   - ◆ A geographical area or region of the country
   - ◆ A daily routine
   - ◆ An art form, such as folk music
   - ◆ A movie or play synopsis

5. Some aspects of the grammar can be used as the basis for a spiel. They would need to be prepared, not spontaneous. For example:

   Verb tenses: Usually I take the bus to school, but yesterday I walked. I will do that more often when the weather is good. Sometimes I have taken a taxi. I had done that quite often when I lived nearby. I think I will have walked quite often by the end of the term. I am planning to take the bus home tonight. In fact, I was planning to take the bus yesterday, but I had forgotten my wallet. If I walk more, I will be getting good exercise.

   Article usage: I bought an apple and a banana. The apple was green; the banana was yellow. An apple is quite nutritious. The banana is a good source of potassium. I also bought some cherries. The cherries were red. (ø) Cherries are my favorite (ø) fruit. I ate all the fruit last night. (ø) Fruit is very good for you.

   Adjective order: I bought a new car. It was red – a new red car. It was beautiful – a beautiful new red car. It was expensive – a beautiful, expensive new red car. It was Japanese – a beautiful expensive new red Japanese car.

Note

This technique is based on one developed by Earl W. Stevick.

Survey

Purpose

To engage the students in a guided but self-directed conversation on a specific topic in a way that keeps them on topic.

Brief Description

The students are given a list of questions on a specific topic – a survey. Frequently the questions ask for opinions or personal information. Either inclass or at home for homework, they write out short notes/answers. Then in a small conversation group they discuss their various responses. The teacher circulates, monitors, and takes notes on errors or problems.

Sample Survey

Pets

In my opinion, having a pet is _____ because _____
_____

Dogs make good/bad pets because _____
_____

Cats make good/bad pets because _____
_____

Pets are good/bad for children because _____
_____

Pets are good/bad for senior citizens because _____
_____

A good pet for someone who lives in an apartment is _____ because
_____

Some problems pets can cause are _____
_____

When I was younger, I had a pet _____. Its name was _____
In my native country, many people have pet _____
I'm annoyed when a pet owner _____
_____

From: *Surveys for Conversation*, Deborah F. Hitsky, Pro Lingua Associates.

Procedure

1. Prepare a one-page questionnaire and give it to the students. Explain the activity.

2. Go through the questions with the students to be sure they understand the questions.

3. Have the students prepare answers to the questions. Although this can be done in class, it may work better as an overnight assignment. The students may give it more thought if they don't have to begin talking right away.

4. Put the class into groups of three or four students.

5. Appoint a group leader for each group. The leader will be responsible for making sure that the group stays on target.

6. The students carry out a discussion based on their surveys. Meanwhile, the teacher circulates, monitoring and taking notes on errors and questions. Establish a time limit to the discussion.

7. In a whole group setting, spokespersons from each group can compare how their conversations went.

Variations

1. The students can create a survey.

2. The students can survey someone who is not in their class and report the results to the class.

3. Tell the students not to put their names on the survey. Collect all the surveys and hand them back to people who did not write the survey. In groups, the students give the information on the surveys and the others try to guess who the original writer is.

4. Set the students up in two circles – inner and outer. The inner circle discusses, and the outer circle takes notes. The notes can be about the content, and at the end of the conversation the outer circle students use reported speech to say who said what. The outer circle can also be listening for errors, and after the conversation, they point them out and discuss them. Then the groups switch roles.

Suggestions and Guidelines for Writing a Survey

1. You may want to precede the conversation with words, phrases, and sentences that are useful in conversation, such as, *Really?* or *In my opinion,* or *I don't agree.* They can be written on a handout or on the board. A one-page copyable handout can be found in *Surveys for Conversation.*

2. Some proven topics:

    ◆ My mother, father, sister, etc.
    ◆ Summer, fall, etc.
    ◆ Food preferences
    ◆ Eating out
    ◆ Clothes
    ◆ Sports
    ◆ Health
    ◆ Housing
    ◆ Dieting
    ◆ Television
    ◆ Music
    ◆ The cinema
    ◆ Travel
    ◆ Dating
    ◆ Weddings
    ◆ The lottery/gambling
    ◆ Vacation
    ◆ Hobbies
    ◆ Technology
    ◆ The environment
    ◆ Crime and punishment
    ◆ Women's rights
    ◆ War
    ◆ Space exploration
    ◆ Predicting the future

3. Current local, national, and international issues can often result in debate.

4. Depending on your circumstances, some topics are best avoided.

Line Up

Purpose

To engage the students in conversation practice as they attempt to solve a problem.

Brief Description

Each student is given a piece of information. Index cards are useful for this. The information is a list that needs to be arranged in an order from most, etc., to least, etc.

Sample Line Up

How Long Does It Take to Decompose?

(Time is not included in student's information.)

paper towel 2–4 weeks

banana peel 3–4 weeks

paper bag 1 month

newspaper 1.5 months

apple core 2 months

cardboard 2 months

orange peel 6 months

plywood, 1–3 years

wool sock 1–5 years

milk carton 5 years

cigarette butt 10–12 years

leather shoe 25–40 years

tin can 50 years

aluminum can 200–500 years

plastic bag 200–1000 years

plastic bottle 450 years – forever

disposable diaper 550 years

Source: www.hoaxorfact.com/science/how-long-does-it-take-to-decompose.html

Procedure

1. Check that the students know the vocabulary of the items that will be arranged.

2. Give each student a card. Ten to twelve different items seem to work best. Make sure the items are distributed in random order. Tell the students what they are supposed to do.

3. Have the students stand up and talk to each other as they arrange themselves in a line, as in the sample above, from shortest to longest biodegradability.

4. Have the students say their items.

5. (optionally, depending on the proficiency of the class) They explain the placement of their item.

6. When they are ready, read the answers.

7. Hold a discussion on "What surprised you?" and "How do you feel about this?"

Variations

1. With a larger class, have two groups of students form two lines. When they are ready have them compare their lines and discuss any differences.

2. With a small class, the students can lay out their cards on a table top or in the chalk/marker tray on the board.

Suggestions and Guidelines for Writing a Line Up

1. This can be an interesting summary activity after a unit on a particular topic, such as the environment.

2. Some possible lists:

   - ◆ cost of items, such as cars or TVs
   - ◆ popularity of websites
   - ◆ distances of places from classroom
   - ◆ the solar system
   - ◆ country/city/state population or electoral votes
   - ◆ Olympic Games results
   - ◆ nutritional value of foods
   - ◆ automobile gas mileage
   - ◆ heights of mountains
   - ◆ lengths of rivers
   - ◆ dates of historical events

Notes

1. Line ups are commonly done as ice breakers. Frequently the list is based on students' height, birthdays from January, distance to home, etc.

2. When you discuss the students' results, it can be useful to give them a handout with the correct list and answers, like the sample.

3. Teaching comparative and superlative grammatical constructions fits very naturally into this technique.

4. The Internet is a good and quick source of information.

Information Gap

Purpose

To have students practice listening and speaking in pairs or small groups to complete a map, chart, or list by asking and answering questions about the missing information or "gap."

Brief Description

Students have some of the same information, such as a basic map of a downtown. Each has information that the other is missing, and a list of items to ask about, for example, the location of the bank.

Sample Information Gap with Town Map

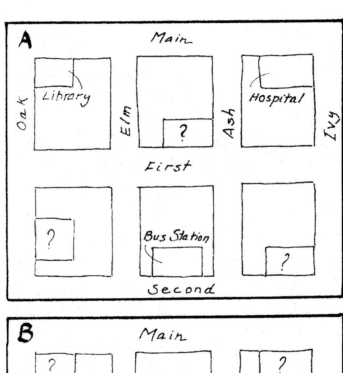

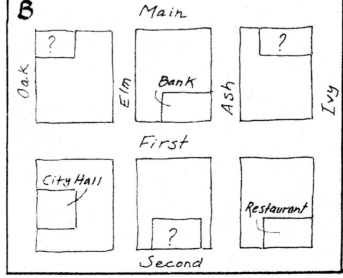

Procedure with map

1. Hand out a complete list of all the items. Review the pronunciation and meanings of the items the students will be asking about. Also, review phrases used to describe location: across from, next to, on the corner of X & Y streets, etc.

2. Pair the students up so that one has Map A and the other Map B. They should not see each other's maps. Give them a minute to study their maps and then direct them to the complete list of locations.

3. When they are ready, they take turns asking questions and completing their maps. Alternatively, without using a list, they can ask: "What's on the corner of Hill Street and West State Street?"

Example:
A asks: *Where is the bank?*
B answers: *It's on the corner of Ash Street and First Street.*

B asks: *Where is the hospital?*
A answers: *It's on the corner of Ivy Street and Main Street.*

4. After the students have filled in the blank spots on their maps, they may confirm their understanding with questions such as the following:
"Is the movie theater next door to the restaurant?"
"The bank is across from the bakery on Main Street, right?"

5. Have the students use the information to write sentences or a summary. This activity may lend itself to comparing and contrasting statements.

Variations

The information gaps may be statistics or figures given in a chart such as:

1. A chart of sports teams and the number of games won or lost this season:
How many games has Boston won so far?
Which team has lost 35 games?

2. A list of students, their colleges, their major and minor fields of study, etc.

A's Chart

Student	College	Major	Minor
Juan		Japanese	Geography
	St. Michael's College		
		Biology	
Ayla	Ohio University		English

B's Chart

Student	College	Major	Minor
	Yale University		
Olivia		Business	Spanish
Ahn	Boston College		none
		Journalism	

3. A list of classic movies showing at different times.

    List A: Gone with the Wind @ 7 PM

    _____ @ 8:45 PM

    List B: _____ @ 7 PM

    King Kong @ 8:45 PM

Suggestions and Guidelines for Writing Information Gap Activities

1. Choose content and structures that students have already encountered, and provide sample starter sentences on the board or on the information sheet:

    Where is the bank?
    What is John's major? What is Kellie's minor?
    Who is studying at Boston College?
    Boston won how many games?/ How many games did Boston win?

    This is especially important for beginners who may still be struggling with structures, vocabulary, and pronunciation as well as production and reception.

2. Ask students for topics they would like or need to practice or have students help create an info gap activity.

Notes

1. When the activity is finished, in many cases the students can discuss the information.

2. The Internet, as well as magazines and newspapers such as *Time* and *USA Today,* can be a good source of graphs and charts.

Dictation

Purpose

To practice listening skills and spelling skills. Incidentally, some vocabulary may be learned and the students will be exposed to grammatical patterns.

Brief Description

Students listen to something that is read or recorded and may be asked to

Complete a gapped text by filling in the missing words (Partial text)
Write an entire dictated sentence
Take notes and write a text

Sample Dictations *(partial text)*

Do you sometimes _____(see)_____ a cigarette butt or a piece of _____

like a candy wrapper on the ground? Cigarette butts are the most littered things

_____ _____ world. Over four trillion cigarette butts are littered_____

_____ world ____ ___ _____ .They last _____ ___ _____

_____ . Most of us like a clean place _____ _____ , so why do

we litter?

From: *Basic Dictations*, Judy DeFilippo and Catherine Sadow. Pro Lingua Associates.

Home on the Range

Oh, give me a _____ where the _____ roam,

Where the deer and the _____ play,

Where _____ is heard a _____ word

And the _____ are not cloudy all day.

Chorus

Home, home on the _____ ,

Where the deer and the antelope play;

Where seldom is _____ a discouraging word

And the _____ are not cloudy all day.

Procedure *(partial text)*

1. Tell the students you are going to read (or play a recording of) a text and you want them to fill in the blanks.

2. Read (play) the text at deliberate speed. Pause if the students are having difficulty.

3. Have pairs check each other's answers.

4. Have volunteers put the answers on the board or on a computer for projection.

5. Have the class read the passage together.

6. Many dictation texts lend themselves to a discussion/conversation follow-up.

Variations

1. Give the students the gapped passage and have them fill it in before listening. Then give the dictation as they listen and self-correct. (prediction dictation)

2. Dictate sentences one at a time as the students simply listen. Then ask them to re-create the sentence as best as they can immediately after they hear it. (dictogloss)

3. Students may benefit from dictating to each other. Create two different gapped passages and have the students dictate to each other. (paired)

4. Dictate a mini-lecture. Have the students take notes and then re-create the passage orally. (note-taking)

5. Dictate a short sentence, phrase by phrase. A recommended pattern is 1) full sentence, 2) syntactic phrases, 3) full sentence.

   There were many deer and antelope on the range. (short pause)
   There were many deer (pause) and antelope (pause) on the range. (pause)
   There were many deer and antelope on the range. (final pause)

6. Short quizzes or riddles can be fun (* indicates pauses):

   1. *I had times * of great sadness *in my life.*
   2. *My mother died * when I was * a young boy.*
   3. *Three of my four sons * died * before age twenty.*
   4. *I failed in business * many times.*
   5. *I lost eight elections * and won only three.*
   6. *I did win * one very important election.*
   7. *I was * the 16ᵗʰ President * of the United States.*
   8. *My name is . . . . (Abraham Lincoln)*

   From: *Dictation Riddles,* Jane Gragg Lewis, Pro Lingua Associates

Suggestions and Guidelines for Writinig a Dictation

1. Texts such as songs, poetry, quotations, sayings, and proverbs can be used to introduce content that can subsequently be discussed for cultural content.

2. Find material that focuses on an area of difficulty, such as hearing and pronouncing the inflection of "-ed" in a sentences. (We handed in our homework.)

3. Reading and/or recording weather forecasts can provide students with a note-taking practice that is iterative and can be done out of class. They can also practice listening to common contractions that are not often taught in textbooks: "The weather for the Boston area'll see temperatures drop… and clouds'll move in …"

4. Look for short news briefs in newspapers and magazines. Especially look for human interest stories that won't date (so you can use them more than once).

Notes

1. If you are using contractions or reductions (should'a, couldja, etc.), practice in class first and review pronunciation and meanings.

2. Pro Lingua publishes five books featuring dictation.

Prose Passage

Purpose

To use a passage of several paragraphs in length as the basis for 1) encountering new language forms, 2) practicing the language by talking about the passage, and 3)(incidentally) learning about the culture.

Brief Description

This technique is basically the same as the age-old practice of teaching the language through the use of readings. However, the recommended procedure as described on page 35 goes beyond reading comprehension, translation, and vocabulary building, the usual practices associated with a prose passage. The emphasis is on building oral-aural skills by using a written passage as a conversation stimulus.

Sample Prose Passage

Dalarna is Sweden's folklore province. Here the bright folk costumes are still worn on festive occasions. Long Viking-style boats race across the lake to church on Sundays. At midsummer the Maypole is joyfully raised in every farm and village. The province is located in central Sweden. It borders on Norway on the west.

The capital is Falun. The Falun coppermine has been designated a World Heritage Site by UNESCO. Dalhalla is an open-air stage, carved out of limestone, with incredible acoustics. In the winter the world's largest cross-country ski race is held. It is called Vasaloppet. More than 15,000 skiers compete in this 90 kilometer race between Salen and Mora.

With a long history of hospitality, Dalarna is now one of Sweden's most popular destinations. Events, activities, relaxation or adventure are enjoyed in unbelievably beautiful natural surroundings and breathtaking views. A red cottage near a beautiful lake, with a deep forest in the distance, is a typical scene in Dalarna. *The New York Times* picked Dalarna as one of the 45 places in the world that we should all visit.

Procedure

1. Read the entire passage once aloud while the students follow along in the book. Then read portions of the passage – perhaps four or five sentences.

2. As you read (slowly) the students should mark words and phrases they don't understand.

3. Have 3 (or 4) students read back to you only the words they have marked.

4. Listen and mark each word or phrase in your text. After the students have given their lists, you will be able to see which words and phrases are probably new to everybody. For example in the sample format, *festive, Viking, midsummer, Maypole,* have been mentioned by at least three students, indicating that it is probably a question for everybody.

5. Define the new words to the class.

6. Have the students define the remaining words to each other by asking each other questions in small groups. Then proceed to the next part of the passage.

Variations

1. Have one or more of the students read the passage aloud.

2. Have the students read the passage silently, marking words and phrases they don't understand. Then have a show of hands to find out which words and phrases gave the most trouble. Read the passage slowly as the students raise their hands when you say new words.

3. After you have worked on the passage intensively, have the students summarize the passage in their own words.

4. Have the students translate the passage.

5. Have a discussion on the subject matter in the passage. If the passage is about some aspect of your culture, you can have a useful discussion on cultural comparison and contrast.

6. Have the students search for and bring to the class passages that are of interest to them.

Suggestions and Guidelines for Writinig a Prose Passage

1. A passage of about one full page or less (double-spaced) would be a good length.

2. Although you can write the passage yourself, it is probably a better practice to find 'real' passages to work with.

3. A good source for these passages would be short entries from the Internet.

4. If you are typing your own passage, double-space it to allow room for marking and writing between the lines.

5. If you have students with dyslexia or attention difficulties, enlarge the font to 14 or 16 point and try printing the passage on pastel paper to reduce the glare of black on white paper. Do this for the whole class so as not to call attention to one student.

Sequence

Purpose

To introduce vocabulary and practice grammatical constructions (especially verb tenses) in the context of a natural or logical sequence of actions.

Brief Description

The students perform and talk about a series of actions that are associated with a process, such as operating a piece of equipment or making something. The sequence can be something repeated on a regular basis in daily life so that each time the student performs the sequence of actions, the words that describe that sequence are available to them for sub-vocalization, or if appropriate, saying aloud.

Sample Sequences

Making a Cup of Tea:

First, boil some water.

Then pour a little into the cup and swirl it around.

Empty the cup and put a tea bag in it.

Pour boiling water into the cup.

Brew the tea 3 to 5 minutes.

Remove the tea bag.

Add sugar, honey, milk, or lemon.

Stir and enjoy your tea!

Getting Money from an ATM:

First, insert your ATM card into the machine.

Enter your PIN (Personal Identification Number)
       and then press Enter.

Select Withdraw Cash.

Enter the amount.

Take the cash and put it in your wallet.

Choose Yes or No for a receipt.

Choose No for another transaction.

Take your card and receipt.

*If you make a mistake, press "Cancel."

Sequence

Procedure

1. Demonstrate the sequence to the students. Go through the entire sequence once without stopping and have the students observe and listen.

2. Go through the sequence again slowly. This time, explain new words.

3. Go through the sequence again while one of the students responds to the commands with the proper action.

4. Teach the students the commands. Have them repeat the sentences several times for practice.

5. Have one of the students give the commands while a second responds with the action. If possible, divide the class into pairs and have each of them practice.

Variations

1. Make a question for each step. After the student has completed the action, ask the question.

    For example:
Teacher:	*Insert your ATM card.*
Student:	(Pretends to insert the card)
Teacher:	*What did you do?*
Student:	*I inserted the card.*

    Note that you will have to teach the students the answer to each question. But you may not need to teach the question and that will allow you to go easily to the next step, which is:

2. Have one student give the command and ask the question while another responds and answers.

3. Have a third student answer the question.

    For example:
1st Student:	*Insert the ATM card.*
2nd Student:	(Pretends to insert the card)
1st Student:	*What did he/she do?*
3rd Student:	*He/she inserted the card.*

4. To help the students keep track of the sequence of actions, put a key word (usually the verb) from each step on the board.

5. After practicing the sequence orally, have the students write it out.

6. Sequences can be very effective review and summary exercises, especially for practicing verb tenses. You could do the following five-tense sequence.

HABITUAL: *What do you do first?*
              First I insert the card.

COMMANDS: *Insert the card.*
              (Inserts the card.)

PRESENT: *What are you doing?*
              I'm inserting the card.

PERFECT: *What have you (just) done?*
              I have inserted the card.

PAST: *What did you do?*
              I inserted the card.

FUTURE: *What are you going to do next?*
              I'm going to enter my PIN.

Suggestions and Guidelines for Writing a Sequence

1. A good length is 6–10 steps (sentences). Keep the sentences as short as possible. A good average is 8 words per line.

2. Sequences provide a good opportunity for practicing discourse connectors such as 'first,' 'next,' 'finally,' 'then,' etc. They also afford a good opportunity for practicing ordinal numbers.

3. Try to choose sequences that the students will frequently encounter in daily life and encourage them to sub-vocalize the sequence whenever they do it.

4. Some possible sequences are:

   ◆ Taking a picture
   ◆ Opening a computer
   ◆ Driving a car
   ◆ Borrowing a book from the library
   ◆ Filling out an application form
   ◆ Planting a garden
   ◆ Sending an email or text message
   ◆ Cooking something with a recipe
   ◆ Downloading an electronic book

Note

For more ideas see: Gayle L. Nelson, Thomas Winters, and Raymond C. Clark, *Do As I Say.* Pro Lingua Associates.

Interview

Purpose

To give the students the opportunity to listen to short pieces of authentic language in a controlled setting. They also have the opportunity to respond appropriately to the flow of the conversation.

Brief Description

The students act as interviewer and one or more native speakers act as interviewees. The students should have a prepared list of questions. The interviewee should respond naturally to the questions, affording the students the opportunity to try to comprehend and respond to natural speech.

Sample Interview Formats

Thank you very much for being with us today.

I'd like to ask you to tell us a bit about yourself.

What is your name?

Where do you live?

Can you tell us about your family?

What do you do?

How long have you done that?

What is your favorite kind of music?

Why do you like_____?

Can you name some of your favorite pieces of _____?

Where can I hear _____?

Who is your favorite performer of _____?

Can you play a musical instrument?

Can you sing a _____ song?

What is your opinion about _____ ?

Why do you think that way?

Have you always had this opinion?

Could you explain that a little more?

What do you mean by _____ ?

Do you agree that _____ ?

Procedure

1. Go over the prepared list of questions with the students to be sure they understand them.

2. Have the students practice saying the questions.

3. Have the students practice the questions while you play the role of interviewee. Try this two or three times, varying your responses. Encourage the students to interrupt, ask for clarifications, repetitions, spellings, definitions, etc.

4. Invite one or more guest interviewees to class and have one student act as interviewer.

5. During the interview the other students should take notes.

6. After the interview hold a question-answer session where the other class members can ask the interviewee questions.

7. Have the class summarize the interviewees' responses.

Variations

1. Have the students prepare their own list of questions.

2. Have the students interview each other for practice.

3. The class can go on an interview field trip rather than bring interviewees to the classroom. Appoint a class recorder who is responsible for collecting new words and phrases that emerge during the conduct of the interview. Students may wish to use an electronic recording device such as a phone or iPad. Remind them to ask permission first and explain that it is to help them work with the language and comprehension skills.

4. Act as the interviewer and interview each of your students.

Suggestions and Guidelines for an Interview

1. Pick a specific subject and limit your questions to fact-finding questions.

2. Try to use all of the major question words with each subject (what, when, where, how, why, who).

3. Match your questions to subject matter areas that the students have some familiarity with.

4. Keep the interviews brief: 6-10 questions.

5. Some possible topics are:

   ◆ Brief biographical information
   ◆ Daily routine
   ◆ Occupations
   ◆ Recreational/vacation preferences
   ◆ Hobbies
   ◆ Talents and skills
   ◆ Sports
   ◆ Ethnic background
   ◆ How to make, cook, operate, perform something
   ◆ Trips and traveling (My trip to Paris)

Note

This technique is a modification of an idea suggested by Dr. Ani Hawkinson and adapted by Phil Sedlak.

Readers' Theater

Purpose

To expose the students to conversations written as plays. The nature of the conversations is usually dramatic and the students will practice being expressive.

Brief Description

Short plays or longer dialogues are the basis for speaking expressively – learning to use stress, intonation, rhythm, etc., dramatically as well as using colloquial language and appropriate conversational discourse.

Sample Readers' Theater Script

Arrival at the Brown's House

Ann and JD, her new husband, arrive at Ann's parents' house. JD meets them for the first time.

Ann: Mom! Dad, we're here! How are you *(embracing them)*? I want you to meet my husband, JD. JD, this is my mother, Catherine, and my father, Tom.

Catherine: *(embracing JD)* My daughter told us what a wonderful man you are. Let me look at you! *(Looking at him, laughing)* You are handsome! Ann, you made a good choice.

Ann: Mom, don't embarrass him.

Tom: *(Tom shakes JD's hand unenthusiastically)* I am very happy to meet you.

JD: And I am happy to meet you, too.

Catherine: Welcome to our home, JD! From now on, our home is your home. Tom?

Tom: *(weakly)* Yes! Of course, of course. Welcome! Welcome!

JD: You two are very kind. Thank you for this warm welcome.

Catherine: Well, it's time to eat! Ann, I have made all your favorites. JD, do you like chicken?

JD: It is my favorite too!

Readers' Theater

Procedure

1. Explain the nature of the activity to the students and give the background for the dramatic reading.

2. Hand out copies of the script and read it to the students, stopping to take and answer questions. At this time it is not necessary to read dramatically.

3. Assign parts. In the sample there are four parts. With a larger class, you can set up groups of four. In some cases students have to share a part or take two parts.

4. Have the students practice reading the script to each other. Listen and help with pronunciation discreetly.

5. After a few practice runs, have one group read the lines. This time, break in and model the phrase and sentences with dramatic delivery.

6. After additional practice in which you circulate and provide dramatic input, have one group "perform" their lines. Encourage them to read a phrase silently, look up, and say it.

Variations

1. Have the students also stand and move around as appropriate.

2. If the script is fairly short, as in the sample, have one group be the performers and another the prompters – one prompter for each performer. The performers do not have the script. This is done after several practice sessions so that the lines are at least familiar to the performers. For example, Ann's first lines:

> Ann (performer): *Mom! Dad, we're here! How are you? I uh...*
> Ann (prompter): *I want you*
> Ann (performer): *I want you to meet my husband, JD. uh...*
> Ann (prompter): *JD, this is*
> Ann (performer): *JD, this is my mother, Catherine, and my father, Tom.*

3. Record the performance and have the students critique it.

4. Have the students create their own script.

Suggestions and Guidelines for Readers' Theater

1. Several publications for ESL students are available, among them:

    Short and Sweet ESL (www.Sharonsbooks.com)

    For more on Readers' Theater see: www.aaronshep.com

    All the World's a Stage (Alta Books)

    Plays for the Holidays (Pro Lingua Associates)

    Celebrating American Heroes (Pro Lingua Associates)

2. Fables and folk tales are a good source of materials for creating short playlets.

3. Check the Internet for foreign language plays such as *Le Sorcier d'Oz*.

4. The sample text is from *Trials and Errors*, 42 long dialogues that relate the life of a young couple, from arrival in the US to their first baby. (Pro Lingua Associates)

5. *A Phrasal Verb Affair* is a soap opera in 15 scenes. (Pro Lingua Associates)

Characters in Search of an Author

Purpose

To practice using the language by talking about representative people from the culture. This technique may also be extended to a role-play format whereby the 'authors' (students) take on the personality of the character, and through the characters engage in dramatic interplay.

Brief Description

Each student is given a picture of a person. The teacher initiates the lesson by giving some information about the person. Each student then provides similar information about their character. The students can then ask and answer questions and talk about each other's characters. This technique can be repeated over several days; each time it is done, new information is added and the characters gradually acquire a biography.

Sample Character Format

This is John Everyman. He is 27 years old. He lives in Erewhon. He is an English teacher.

(The categories could be written on the back of the picture. Each student writes in the facts for each category. Then each student would make a short statement such as the model above.)

Name:

Age:

Resident of:

Occupation:

Characters in Search of an Author

Procedure

1. Give every student (and yourself) a picture of a character.

2. Hold up your own picture and describe it with a few sentences.

3. Ask and answer questions after every sentence.

4. Tell the students to make up similar information about their own characters. It may be best to have the students write down the information (perhaps on the back of the picture). Then you can check the accuracy and cultural appropriateness of your students' sentences. For example, a student might say that an 18-year old woman lives alone, when in fact, this would never happen in the target culture. These mistakes can be used as an opportunity to discuss your culture.

5. Each student in turn describes their character.

6. Ask the students questions about the characters. For example:

1st Student:	*He is 18 years old.*
Teacher:	*How old is he?*
2nd Student:	*He is 18 years old.*

7. Ask each student to describe somebody else's character.

Variations

1. At the beginning of the lesson, write your model sentences on the board for the students to refer to when they create their own sentences.

2. Have the students speak for their characters. They would then practice 'I' and 'you' as well as 'he/she.'

3. As a final step, switch all the pictures and ask the students to describe their new character. If they cannot remember the correct information they must then ask the originator for it.

4. Set up a role-play situation (see Role-Play, p. 57) and have the characters interact with each other.

5. Pose a problem to the class and ask each student to express their character's opinion about the problem. Local and international current events would be a good source for these problems.

6. Periodically have the students write out in narrative form the biographies that are being developed.

7. This technique should be carried out over several days so that biographies can develop. Try it for 20 minutes a day for at least two weeks. By asking the students to assume the identity of their own characters, you may notice that this has a liberating effect on your students. They may be more willing to make mistakes, express opinions, and interact in a dramatic fashion. Note that some students—those with Asperger's Syndrome, an Autism Spectrum Disorder—may find it difficult to assume another identity or to read or engage in appropriate social behavior. A reminder that they are taking on the role of an actor as in a play or film can sometimes help them bridge the gap. If not, it may still be useful for them to talk about their character in the third person.

Suggestions and Guidelines for Developing Characters

1. Magazines are a good source for pictures. Cut them out and paste them on stiff paper or cardboard.

2. Choose a variety of people, although it may be best to have characters that the students can readily identify with.

3. Listed below are some of the categories that you could use in describing the characters. In general, 3-5 items should be sufficient for any one lesson.

◆ name	◆ occupation
◆ age	◆ salary
◆ birthday	◆ educational level
◆ place of birth	◆ religion
◆ nationality	◆ hobbies
◆ language	◆ sports
◆ ethnic group	◆ interests
◆ family	◆ friends
◆ residence	◆ political beliefs
◆ personality traits	◆ hopes and dreams

4. Pro Lingua publishes a book called *Faces, Characters in Search of an Author* by Pat Moran. It is a collection of 50 full-page drawings of faces of people of different ages. They can be photocopied.

Constructalog

Purpose

To involve students directly in the content of the language class by giving them the opportunity to write their own dialogues. By trying to write their material, the students will also encounter linguistic problems that might stimulate questions and investigations into the language.

Brief Description

The students are given pieces of language (words, phrases, and sentences) and asked to create a dialogue by using these pieces. Usually this is done with the students working in pairs or in small groups.

Sample Constructalog Formats

A. Use the words and phrases below to construct a dialogue between a sick person and a doctor. You do not need to use every word.

hurt	fever
pain	take a pill
ache	take temperature
stomach	give an injection/shot
headache	feel

B. Use the words and phrases below to construct a dialogue between a mother and a child. Try to use every word.

put away

toys

a nap

not tired

C. (No list provided) Construct a dialogue between a 911 operator and a person who sees some suspicious activity.

Procedure

1. Go over the list of words and phrases with the students to be sure they understand them and have some idea of how to use them. Have the students say a sentence using each word or phrase.

2. After the students understand the key words and phrases have them work individually or in small groups to write the dialogue.

3. Check each dialogue as it is being written. Point out errors and help the students, but don't be too obtrusive. The students should be allowed to make errors as they work; they can learn a lot from their mistakes.

4. Have the students practice their dialogues in pairs or small groups.

5. Have each group present its dialogue to the rest of the class.

Variations

1. Don't provide a word list; let the students develop their dialogues from scratch. However, in order to keep the class as a whole focused on one semantic area, it may be best to give the class a topic, situation, or problem to start with.

2. After each group has prepared and presented a dialogue, have the groups exchange dialogues and practice a new one.

3. Choose one of the dialogues and write it on the board. Have everyone practice it.

4. Have each group dictate its dialogue to the rest of the class so that everyone gets a copy of everyone else's work. Or have each group email or provide an electronic copy for the class.

Suggestions and Guidelines for a Constructalog

1. About 12 words would be sufficient to guide the students in writing their own dialogues.

2. Have the students limit their dialogue to 12 or fewer lines.

3. Choose topics, situations, and problems that will be relevant to the students.

4. Some possible dialogue situations are:

   - at a bank
   - at a post office
   - at a theatre box office
   - at a doctor's office
   - in a store
   - in a restaurant
   - at a gas station
   - at a bus station
   - in a police station
   - in a bar
   - in a taxi
   - at customs/immigration

Notes

1. The basic idea of this technique, having the students write their own material, can be extended to other formats besides a dialogue.

2. This technique should not be attempted until the students have some familiarity with the language. They should use the target language, not their native language, as they work together preparing the material.

3. Pictures could also be used. Comic strips with the dialogue in the balloons deleted are one possibility.

4. *Talkabouts*, published by Pro Lingua, is a book of pictures withour words. Some are series of pictures of common situations (shopping, visiting, etc.) and some are scenes.

Role-Play

Purpose

To put the students into a realistic communication situation to 1) sharpen their listening comprehension skills, 2) bring them in contact with their new language, and 3) discover areas where they need additional practice.

Brief Description

There is no pre-established language sample for this technique, only a set of instructions that initiates a conversation. Often the conversation/role-play is between the teacher and one or more students.

Sample Role-Play Situations

You have just moved into your new apartment and your neighbor knocks on your door to introduce him/herself.

Ask for directions to the nearest supermarket.

You and your friend want to meet at a restaurant for dinner. Decide where and how to get there.

You are not feeling well and you need to ask your boss for permission to go home.

Your friend is drinking a little too much at a party. Tell them to cool it.

Your friend wants to get their nose pierced. Give them your opinion.

Your house is infested with fleas. Call the landlady and ask her to do something about it.

Your friend wants to fly to the Caribbean, but you are afraid of flying. Talk to them about it.

You believe that a student is constantly playing video games and becoming obese because they are not exercising. Talk to the parent.

You are at an airport. Your baggage has just arrived, but it is damaged. Go ask for compensation at the baggage claim office.

You are at a movie theater. The people behind you are making a lot of noise. Talk to them.

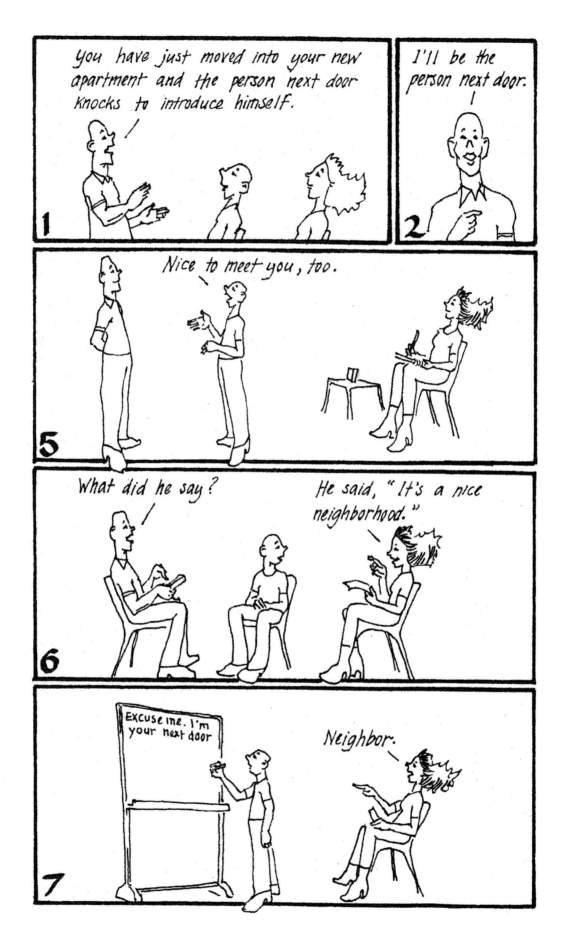

Procedure

1. Explain the situation.

2. Select the "cast." Depending on the proficiency level of the students, initially, it may be best to cast yourself in one of the key roles.

3. If a voice or video recorder is available, have one of the students record the role-play.

4. Have the other students take notes. A simple system is to have the note-takers construct a log of the conversation, noting only the opening words of each new line and, if possible, the last word of each line (See Notes).

5. Role-play the situation. Try to let it develop naturally. Don't let it go on too long: one or two minutes is sufficient.

6. Play the recording. Pause after each utterance for questions and answers. If the students don't have any questions, ask simple questions such as "*What did he say?*"

7. Gradually re-construct a written version of the role-play, using the recording and/or the log.

Variations

1. Have students develop a situation and do the role-play while you listen for errors and take notes. Do not interrupt the role-play while it is in progress. Afterward, or during a replay, comment on and correct the students' sentences.

2. After doing the role-play once, select a new cast and do it again. Have one of the students take your role.

3. Add a new element to the instructions, one that will force the role-play to take a slightly different direction.

4. Discuss any cross-cultural communication problems that may have arisen during the role-play.

5. Combine this technique with *Characters in Search of an Author* (see p. 49).

Suggestions and Guidelines for Developing a Role-Play

1. Be careful that the role-play doesn't go on too long. Too much material can overload the student with too many new words, phrases, and constructions. Students can only deal with a limited number of new pieces of information at one sitting.

2. Some possible role-play situations are:

   ◆ a social visit in a home
   ◆ interviewing a job applicant
   ◆ asking to borrow something
   ◆ turning down an invitation gracefully
   ◆ a visit to a doctor or dentist
   ◆ firing an employee
   ◆ reporting a stolen or lost item
   ◆ helping an accident victim or sick person
   ◆ accepting a ride as a hitch-hiker
   ◆ returning a defective item to a store

Notes

To facilitate the keeping of a role-play log, use a form like the one below to help keep track of the flow of the conversation.

Line #	VISITOR (teacher)	HOST (Raoul)	
1	Excuse me ... neighbor.		
2		Hello ... come in.	
3	My name ... Brown.		
4		My name ... Smith.	
5	Nice to meet ..		

Storytelling

Purpose

To help the students develop their discourse skills by relating a long passage in which there is some kind of beginning, middle, and end with appropriate discourse connectors throughout. A secondary purpose is to encourage the students to be expressive and engaging as they speak.

Brief Description

A variety of textual material may be used with this technique. Folktales are one good source. Other possibilities include short bio-sketches, anecdotes, jokes, brief news stories, and even on-line encyclopedia-type entries.

Sample Stories for Telling

The Horse and the Donkey

A fat and lazy horse was traveling with a heavily loaded donkey and their owner. The donkey was sick, and its back was breaking. It begged the horse to help carry the load. But the lazy horse refused.

A little farther down the road, the donkey fell down and died. The owner then threw the donkey's load on the horse's back and on top of that, the dead donkey.

From *Story Cards: Aesop's Fables*, Pro Lingua Associates.

You Don't Believe Me

One day a friend came to Hodja's house to borrow a donkey. "I'm sorry," said Hodja, "but I've already lent it to someone else." Just then the donkey made a loud noise from the back of the house.

"Hodja, " the man said, "I just heard your donkey! It's out back." Angrily, Hodja asked his friend to leave the house.

"What kind of friend are you?" he said. "You believe my donkey, but you don't believe me!"

From *Nasreddin Hodja, Stories to Read and Retell*, Pro Lingua Associates.

Procedure

1. Tell the students a "story" the first time you use this technique. They simply listen. Discuss how you told it. You can point out how *a* shifts to *the*, and how the opening line sets the stage, how *the donkey* becomes *it*, and how *but* is an important connector.

2. Give each student a different story and ask them to study it. As they study their stories, circulate to help with vocabulary or meaning.

3. Tell the students that when they think they can tell (not read) the story, they should stand up and find another person who is standing.

4. The two "tellers" tell their stories to each other. Then they look again at the story to see if they got it right and to see how they might improve the next time.

5. When they are finished, they split and find another person to tell their stories to.

6. This continues until they are telling their stories quite fluently.

Variations

1. After the two tellers have told each other their stories, they help each other practice and learn each other's story. Then they spit and find another person and swap stories. This can be fairly challenging.

2. With lower proficiency students, you can give everyone the same story. Have pairs practice telling each other the story, and then ask for a volunteer to tell the story to the whole class. Alternatively, the pair can take turns telling the story sentence by sentence.

3. Give a story to a group that has the same number of members as characters in the story. After practicing, the group presents their story to the class. One member reads it, and the others act and speak the lines in the story.

Suggestions and Guidelines for Developing Stories for Telling

1. Choose passages that can easily fit on index cards. For lower proficiency students, a standard index card. For tose with higher proficiency, a large (5 x 8) index card.

2. If you copy and paste the story on one side, you can write key words as they appear sequentially in the story on the backside as prompts.

Notes

1. For sources of folk tales, check Pro Lingua's *How and Why Folktales* (worldwide), *Nasreddin Hodja* (Turkish; Middle East), *The Dragons Without Eyes* (Chinese), *Pearls of Wisdom* (West African and Caribbean – longer and more challenging), and *North American Indian Tales*.

2. Bio-sketches can also be used with this technique. See *Real Lives* and *Legends* from Pro Lingua.

3. Many newspapers have short news summaries.

4. Reader's Digest has anecdotes and jokes.

5. Wikipedia can be a source for encylopedia entries.

Valuations

Purpose

To stimulate conversation practice using subject matter which is of high interest to the students. The conversations may also be controversial.

Brief Description

The students are asked to state their likes (or dislikes) in the form of a simple list. Then they compare and talk about their lists.

Sample Valuations Format

A: List your five favorite TV programs, starting with your first choice.

1. _____
2. _____
3. _____
4. _____
5. _____

B: Use the grid to list your and your classmates' five favorite TV programs.

	1	2	3	4	5
Teacher					
Jon					
Kathy					
Susannah					

Valuation

Procedure

1. Present the question to the students. A simple kind of valuation activity is to ask the students to: List your five favorite _____s.

2. Allow the students time to think about and construct their lists.

3. Have each person (you can include yourself) simply read their list while the others listen.

4. Have the students ask and answer questions and discuss each other's lists.

5. Listen for words and phrases that the students need or can't handle properly. Note them down, slip them into the discussion wherever possible, and call the students' attention to them when the discussion is over.

Variations

1. Have the students suggest topics for valuation.

2. Have the students put their lists on the blackboard for quick reference.

3. After each student reads their list, have another re-state it. This will focus attention on the need to listen carefully.

4. Keep a few notes as the lists are being read and then quiz everyone briefly with questions such as:

   Who likes _____?
   Does Juan like _____?
   Does anybody like _____?
   How many people like _____?

5. Have each student construct a grid (see Sample Format) to record everyone's list.

6. At the end of the discussion have each student write a short summary of the discussion.

Suggestions and Guidelines for Developing Valuations

1. If the activity goes slowly, try reducing the list to three items. This may be especially necessary with larger classes. Keep in mind that the activity can be overwhelmed by too much information.

2. Some possible lists are:
   - ◆ food/drinks/restaurants
   - ◆ books/magazines/authors
   - ◆ movies/movie stars
   - ◆ cities/states, countries
   - ◆ TV programs/TV stars
   - ◆ hobbies/interests
   - ◆ sports/sports teams
   - ◆ academic subjects
   - ◆ pieces of music
   - ◆ automobiles
   - ◆ politicians

3. It is probably best to start with items that are not too controversial. However, with advanced classes the discussions can be very heated and challenging. An old classic is the "too many people in the lifeboat" activity.

Note

The valuation list described as the basis for this technique is only one very simple activity based on the practice of values clarification. Google for more information on the practice. An old but useful introduction is: *Values Clarification*, by Sidney B. Simon, Leland W. Howe, and Howard Kirschenbaum.

Community Survey

Purpose

In a teaching context in which the target language is spoken outside the classroom, this is a particularly useful and enjoyable activity for students to do at the beginning of a program. It helps them get to know a broad spectrum of the community quickly, and to get to know and bond with their classmates by working with them. Additionally, it provides them with an opportunity to speak the language in a real situation right from the beginning. With specific tasks in mind, the students can control and predict language they may hear and may need to produce.

Brief Description

Students are sent in pairs or small groups to explore various aspects of the community. (In larger cities, the "community" may be a neighborhood or section of the city.) They brainstorm beforehand what they are going to look for (posters, bulletin boards, flyers, phone books, people on the street). They then establish certain aspects of the community to be researched by pairs or small groups. To help them organize their research, they can be given a questionnaire like the sample below. They gather information and finally they share and summarize their information back in the classroom.

Sample Town Survey

Specific survey questions will differ from place to place. Below are some possible questions.

1. What are the names of the principal streets? Create a street map.

2. Where is (are) the local government building(s)?

3. How many places to eat are there? What kinds are they?

4. What kinds of stores are there? What kinds aren't there?

5. Is there a library? Are other public places such as schools? banks? a police station? a courthouse? churches – which denominations? mosques? synagogues? parks? a senior center? a post office?

6. How does the community look? Pretty? Dull? Interesting? Busy? Quiet?

7. How do people feel about their community?

8. Who are the local community leaders?

9. What is distinctive about the community?

Community Survey

Procedure

1. Work with the students to develop a list of research topics or give them a questionnaire about the community they will survey.

2. Have the students brainstorm how to collect information -- taking photographs, making sketches and maps, bringing back relevant brochures/flyers, talking to people, etc.

3. Review interviewing techniques, including introductions and leave-takings, and have the students practice.

4. Have the students work in pairs or small groups to decide who will research what, and who will take notes on (or record) the interviews. Their focus could be to learn about one aspect of the community in detail with a class goal to create a mini-guide for the community.

5. Send the students out to carry out the research. Give them a time limit. You may want to inform local authorities about this project.

6. After the research give the students time to review their notes or other resources and time to prepare a presentation to the larger group.

7. Depending on the class and group size, have the pairs or a group representative present findings. The class should ask questions for clarification if needed.

8. Debrief by asking the whole class:

   What do you now know about the community that you didn't know before?

   What surprised you?

   What was funny or unusual?

   How was your experience doing such a survey?

   Did you learn any vocabulary?

   What difficulties did you have?

Variations

1. This activity can also be used later in the program after the students have identified and studied local issues and aspects of the community, such as:

   How do you feel about nuclear power?

   How was the town different 20 years ago? 50 years ago?

   Where was the first settlement in the community?

   What artifacts remain in the community that suggest some of its history? (Mound Park, the Scioto Trail, Mill Street, Cotton Mill Hill, etc.)

2. Have the students ask the same questions in different parts of the community and then compare answers. Discuss how they might confirm the accuracy of their results.

3. Have the students record their interviews with a digital device (phone, recorder, iPad, etc.) after asking permission.

4. Have the students write a summary or guide to the community.

Suggestions and Guidelines for a Community Survey

1. For beginners, limit the survey to simple questions and send students out in pairs or groups of three or four. More advanced students may want to go alone or in pairs.

2. Engage the students in planning the topics they will explore, so that they will be invested in the activity.

3. Help the class predict and practice the vocabulary and structures they may need to use or understand.

4. Remind the students to spread out and avoid having one group after another approach the same shop or people.

5. Send a note of thanks (written by students if possible) to the businesses or places they visited.

Impromptu

Purpose

To give advanced-level students the opportunity to use the language they have been learning in a relatively free assignment. They will also develop teamwork skills as they put together a skit.

Brief Description

The students are given an open-ended scene which sets the stage for an event. Working as a team they create a skit/mini-drama, practice it, and bring the scene to a dramatic conclusion as a presentation to the rest of the class – or to you, the teacher.

Sample Impromptu

You and your friend are in your car coming home after a pleasant day at the beach. It is dark, and you have taken a shortcut through a quiet stretch of a secondary road with very few houses. You turn the corner and you see in the headlights someone signaling you to stop. There are no houses visible, and there is no car beside the road. As you approach, they signal more desperately. They are trying to tell you something. You begin to slow down. You come to a stop and your friend rolls down the window.

Instructions: Option A. In a group of four, discuss the situation and decide on a plot. Practice it at least once outside the classroom and then present it to the rest of the class.

Instructions: Option B. In two groups of three or four, Group A (you and your friend) and Group B (the person in the road) discuss the situation separately, and then enact the situation. One of you in Group A begins with "Look! Who is that?"

Instructions to observers. Listen to the impromptu and note any grammar or vocabulary questions you might have. When the impromptu is over, discuss it with the cast.

Procedure

1. Describe the nature of the impromptu to the class, and give them the scene.

2. Ask the class to read and understand the scene. There may be some vocabulary problems.

3. Depending on the nature of the impromptu, put the students into groups and have them develop a story line. You may want to set a time limit.

4. If more than one group will perform, give the non-performing observers an assignment, such as to listen for errors or new words.

5. Have the students perform the impromptu as others watch.

6. After all groups have performed, have everyone critique the performances.

Variations

1. You can have groups perform different scenes.

2. The sample scene is written for three students. You can write scenes for four or five, but more than five can be confusing and difficult to manage. You can write scenes even for solo performers.

3. After the performance the observers can retell the scene as a narrative.

4. After the performance the students can pose as reporters interviewing the performers.

5. The students can create their own scenes.

6. Have the students read a short story (O. Henry is a good source) or a long folk tale and then perform it.

Suggestions and Guidelines for Writing an Impomptu

1. Keep the scene fairly short, and try to leave it with an unanswered question or solution.

2. Groups of three to four work very well.

Note

Improvisation for Creative Language Practice by Lou Spaventa (Pro Lingua) has 44 scenes for one to six performers.

Minimal Pair Exercise

Purpose

To help students hear and say two sounds (segments) that are difficult for them to differentiate.

Brief Description

Two columns of words are arranged on the board or screen or poster as in the sample below. The words in the two columns are almost identical except for one sound in each word that is different. The differing sounds are selected because the learners are having difficulty with one or both sounds.

Samples

Vowels

/ I /	/ EE /	/U/	/OO/
1	2	1	2
bit	beet	pull	pool
live	leave	stood	stewed
ship	sheep	look	Luke
rich	reach	wood	wooed
sit	seat	full	fool
is he	easy	should	shooed

Consonants

/th/	/T/	/R/	/L/
1	2	1	2
thin	tin	rice	lice
threw	true	rate	late
theme	team	right	light
Beth	bet	race	lace
bath	bat	pour	pole
both	boat	berry	belly

The symbols for the sounds are from Pro Lingua's phonemic alphabet (page 80).

Minimal Pair Exercise

Procedure

1. Introduce the activity by showing how the sounds are made. Exaggeration is helpful at this stage.

2. Begin the practice by saying the words in Column 1 as the students listen. Then say the words in Column 2 as they listen.

3. Say the words across the columns: "beet .. bit."

4. Be careful to use the same intonation on each word.

5. Say the words randomly, asking the students to respond with either "one" or "two," indicating which sound they hear. Alternative: they can hold up one or two fingers.

6. Have the students repeat after you. First, column one; then column two; then across the columns.

7. Point at a word and have the students say it.

8. Have individuals say the words as you point to them.

Variations

1. The pairs could be presented in phrases or sentences after the practice.
   For example: *Which one is correct, one or two?*

He beat the dog.	*He bit the dog.*
She deed it.	*She did it.*
How do you feel?	*How do you fill?*
I hurt my heap.	*I hurt my hip.*

2. It is possible to do minimal trios.

Suggestions and Guidelines for Writing Minimal Pairs

1. Consult a book or other source that will indicate which sounds will be difficult for learners from different linguistic backgrounds.
2. Although a board is a handy way to show the pairs, if you use poster paper and save it in the classroom, you can pull it out and use it as students mispronounce (and one practice is never enough).

Notes

1. For a collection of minimal pairs see *Pronunciation Practice* (Pro Lingua).
2. For more information on teaching pronunciation, try *Teaching North American English Pronunciation* (Pro Lingua),
3. For a book that describes pronunciation problems in English for learners from several different languages see *Learner English* (Cambridge University Press).

Tactics

PLA Phonemic Alphabet

VOWELS   CONSONANTS

SYMBOL	SOUND	SYMBOL	SOUND
EE	beet	M	may
I	bit	B	bay
AI	bait	P	pay
E	bet	W	way
A	bat	HW	whey
ER	her	V	vee
UH	but	F	fee
uh	abut	TH	thy
OO	boot	th	thigh
U	put	N	new
O	boat	D	dew
AW	bought	T	too
AH	pot	L	loo
OU	how	Z	zoo
AY	buy	S	sue
OY	boy	Y	you
		R	rue
		ZH	measure
		SH	show
		J	Joe
		CH	chew
		NG	bang
		G	bag
		K	back
		H	hack.

ADDITIONAL TROUBLESOME PAIRS

VOWELS   CONSONANTS

standard spelling		PLA phonemic spelling		standard spelling		PLA phonemic spelling	
wait	wet	WAIT	WET	pig	big	PIG	BIG
men	man	MEN	MAN	boat	vote	BOT	VOT
cap	cup	KAP	KUHP	lice	rice	LAYS	RAYS
map	mop	MAP	MAHP	cheap	sheep	CHEEP	SHEEP
buck	book	BUHK	BUK	jeep	sheep	JEEP	SHEEP
but	boat	BUHT	BOT	jet	yet	JET	YET
full	fool	FUL	FOOL	death	debt	DEth	DET
toast	tossed	TOST	TAWST	they	day	THAI	DAI
				fine	vine	FAYN	VAYN
				vine	wine	VAYN	WAYN

Sort and Stack

Purpose

To help students distinguish between various aspects of word forms, grammaticality, or pronunciation.

Brief Description

The students are given a set of cards with words on them and asked to "stack" them into piles that have the same characteristic, such as the number of syllables in the word.

Sample (Number of Syllables)

After creating a set such as the one below, copy it, cut it up, paste it on card stock, and then shuffle. The set can be stored in an envelope.

PLATYPUS	KANGAROO	PRAYING MANTIS
CHINCHIILLA	ELEPHANT	CHIPMUNK
VAMPIRE BAT	PANDA	COATIMUNDI
SALAMANDER	GORILLA	TYRANNOSAURUS
MOSQUITO	JACKAL	HIPPOPOTAMUS
RABBIT	CRICKET	GIRAFFE
ARMADILLO	RHINOCEROS	CHIMPANZEE

Procedure

1. Divide the students into groups, having **prepared a set of cards similar to the sample for each.** The sets are cut up and shuffled. It is helpful to use a different color of paper for each set to differentiate between them.

2. Explain the nature of the activity. For the sample: "You are going to put the names of several animals into four piles, depending on whether the name has two, three, four, or five syllables."

3. Give each group of students a set of cards. Pairs or trios work best, although the activity can be done by individuals if you have enough sets of cards. More than 40 cards in a set gets to be a bit tedious.

4. Allow the students to work in their groups.

5. When all have finished, compare results.

6. This game can be played in two stages. After the first sorting, tell the students to rearrange the cards according to which syllable has the primary stress: first, second, third, or fourth.

7. Compare results.

The solution:
Number of syllables

2 syllables	3 syllables	4 syllables	5 syllables
rabbit	platypus	praying mantis	hippopotamus
panda	mosquito	rhinoceros	tyrannosaurus
jackal	elephant	salamander	coatimundi
cricket	gorilla	armadillo	
chipmunk	chimpanzee		
giraffe	vampire bat		
	chinchilla		
	kangaroo		

Stress Placement

1st syllable	2nd syllable	3rd syllable	4th syllable
rabbit	giraffe	chimpanzee	tyrannosauros
panda	mosquito	kangaroo	coatimundi
jackal	gorilla	hippopotamus	
cricket	rhinoceros	armadillo	
chipmunk	chinchilla	praying mantis	
platypus		vampire bat	
elephant			
salamander			

Sort and Stack

Variations:

1. Other pronunciation activities are:
   1) nouns or verbs that are pronounced /S/ as in *books*, /Z/ as in *pens*, or /uhZ/ as in *watches*
   2) regular past tense endings /T/, /D/, /ID/
   3) sound-spelling challenges: /E/, /I/, /EE/ as in *bed, bid, bead*

2. A lexical activity can be based on parts of speech: noun, verb, or adjective. Affixation can be the basis for an activity with prefixes or affixes. For example, a set of words to be affixed with negative prefixes: un-, im-, mis-, or words that have these noun affixes: -ion, -ation, -ment.

3. Grammar sorts can be done with the following:

   A. Stative verbs   Statives and Copulas   Dynamic verbs
       like   *seem*   *write*

   B. intransitive verbs   transitive verbs   intransitive or transitive
       go   *buy*   *get*

   C. intransitive phrasal verb   transitive separable   transitive inseparable
       catch on (understand)   *call up* (phone)   *call on* (visit)

   D. collocations with:

make	*do*	*take*
the bed	the dishes	a shower
a bet	homework	notes

Suggestions and Guidelines for Writing Sort and Stack

1. These activities can all be done using index cards. It's a good idea to put each set on a different color card to keep them from getting mixed up.

2. Part of the value of this activity is that the students should speak with each other. In other words they are practicing conversation as they work. In classes that are monolingual, guard against use of the native language.

3. For working on affixation, consult *Getting a Fix on Vocabulary* (Pro Lingua).

4. For multisyllable words at a lower proficiency level, consult *The Language Learners Lexicon* (Pro Lingua).

5. For working on phrasal verbs, consult *A Phrasal Verb Affair* (Pro Lingua).

6. For grammar, consult *The English Teacher's Grammar* (Cambridge University Press).

7. For questions about the pronunciation of individual words, some students may be more comfortable going to on-line dictionaries such as the *American Heritage Dictionary* (http://ahdictionary.com).

Stress Practice

Purpose

To help students hear differences in stress and intonation patterns, and to understand how stress placement and intonation can change the meaning of the utterance.

Brief Description

This practice is in two parts. In Part A they identify stress placement at the word level; in Part B they identify the meaning of a sentence as stress moves from one word to another (emphatic stress).

Part A (word level stress)

1. Create a list of multisyllable words that have primary stress on different syllables.

2. Tell the students what they are supposed to do (identify the syllable with strongest stress). One easy way is to have them hold up one finger for strongest stress on the first syllable, two fingers for the second syllable, three for the third syllable, and so on.

3. Say the words and have the students identify the stress placement.

Sample Word List

accident	advisor	classify
adventure	artificial	calendar
appointment	association	classification
afternoon	ambulance	congratulations
application	balance	explanation
adjective	boundary	energy
advertise	certificate	exploration
arrival	cigarette	grammatical
attractive	congratulate	immigration

Part B 1 (hearing emphatic stress at phrase/sentence level)

1. Demonstrate how stress placement in a sentence can alter the meaning of the sentence. A short sentence like the sample can be effective. Start from the last word and move toward the first.

> I don't know where she **lives**.
> I don't know where **she** lives.
> I don't know **where** she lives.
> I don't **know** where she lives.
> I **don't** know where she lives.
> **I** don't know where she lives.

2. Have the students listen to the sentences and decide what each sentence means.

Tactics

Sample

1. I don't know what <u>she</u> said.
2. I don't <u>know</u> what she said.
3. I don't know <u>what</u> she said.
4. <u>I</u> don't know what she said.
5. I <u>don't</u> know what she said.
6. I don't know what she <u>said</u>.

Part B 2 (producing emphatic stress at phrase/sentence level)

1. Put a sentence like the sample below on the board.

2. Tell the students that when you say "one" they say the sentence stressing the first word, etc.

Sample

1	2	3	4	5	6	7
I	don't	know	where	he	saw	her.

Part B 3 (producing meaning-based stressed sentences)

1. Create a series of sentences like the sample.

2. Explain the nature of the activity and put a sentence on the board such as "Yoshi speaks Spanish very well." Give an example, such as:

Teacher
Yoshi doesn't speak Arabic very well.

Student(s)
Yoshi speaks **Spanish** very well.

Sample

1. He doesn't read it.
2. He doesn't speak Arabic.
3. He doesn't speak poorly.
4. It isn't Yuko.
5. He doesn't speak French.
6. He doesn't write it.
7. Ahmed doesn't speak Spanish.

A. Yoshi **speaks** Spanish very well.
B. Yoshi speaks **Spanish** very well.
C. Yoshi speaks Spanish **very well**.
D. **Yoshi** speaks Spanish very well.
E. Yoshi speaks **Spanish** very well.
F. Yoshi **speaks** Spanish very well.
G. **Yoshi** speaks Spanish very well.

Intonation Practice

Purpose

To help students hear and produce basic intonation patterns and understand how intonation can affect meaning.

Brief Description

Three exercises are described below for helping the students recognize (1) three levels of pitch, (2) final sentence/phrase intonation, and (3) question intonation patterns.

A. Pitch (Intonation) Levels

1. Have the students sing a short song. "Row, Row, Row Your Boat" works quite well or "Twinkle, Twinkle, Little Star" or the first part of "Three Blind Mice." Call their attention to the three pitch/stress levels.

2. Put together a list of multisyllable words and have the students "sing" the words. Point out how stress and pitch work together.

Sample Word List

defend	declaration	dormitory	distance
division	decide	digitial	dictation
dictator	December	disagree	democracy
destruction	dictionary	department	disease
dangerous	education	demonstration	development

B. Final Sentential/Phrasal Intonation

1. To demonstrate final intonation, construct a chart like the one below.

2. Give the students three examples of a short sentence that ends with (1) falling (statement), (2) rising (question), and (3) mid final intonation (an indication that the speaker has not finished).

Examples: She is a teacher.

She is a teacher?

She is a teacher ...

3. Explain how intonation is the word we use to describe the music of a phrase or sentence. The intonation in a sentence may rise, stay level, fall, rise, etc., etc., and at the end of a sentence or phrase there are three basic intonation patterns: falling, rising, and mid.

   A falling pattern means "I am finished with my thought." (Arrow down)
   A rising pattern means "Will you respond to my question?" (Arrow up)
   A mid pattern means "I have not finished my thought, and . . ." (Arrow suspended)

4. Read each line below five times, each time varying the final intonation. For example, first box, "She's a very good doctor." Second box, "She's a very good doctor?" Third box, "She's a very good doctor . . ." etc. Tell the students to listen to these sentences and decide if the final intonation is falling, rising, or mid. They write F, R, or M in the box as in the first sentence.

Sample

	1	2	3	4	5
She's a very good doctor	F	R	M		
You don't understand					
The dictionary is lost					
They're from Australia					
It's three o'clock					

C. Question Intonation

1. Demonstrate how yes/no questions usually rise and WH questions usually fall. Create some sentences. First say a senteence, and then ask the students to say "rising" or "falling" when you finish the sentence. (Triplets work well.)

Samples (*read across*)

Is she a teacher?	Yes, she is.	What does she teach?
Are they in Boston?	No, they aren't.	Where are they?
He's from Hanoi.	Where is Hanoi?	Don't you know?
Who is teaching history 101?	Isn't it Dr. Gomez?	No, not this year.
How did you do on the exam?	I did OK.	Did you do well?
I am leaving tomorrow.	Why are you going?	Don't you know?
Whose laptop is that?	It is Burak's.	Did he forget it?
The bus leaves in half an hour.	Does it really?	When do you think it leaves?
Is the library open?	What time is it?	It's ten o'clock.
I bought a new cell.	How much did you pay?	Why are you asking?

Intonation Exercise

Slot Substitution Practice

Purpose

To help students develop sentence word order and a particular sentence pattern or grammatical construction by forcing the repetition of the basic sentence while at the same time producing semantic variations of the sentence by changing some part of it.

Brief Description

The teacher says the basic sentence (frame) and adds a word that is to be substituted (cue) in the proper place in the sentence. There are several varieties of substitutions. In some kinds the substitution item forces a change elsewhere in the sentence (indefinite article "a" vs "an" as in the single slot example below, subject-verb agreement, singular-plural agreement, gender agreement). In another major variety, sometimes called the multiple slot substitution practice, there is more than one kind of word being substituted.

Samples of Slot Substitution Practice

A. Single-slot

I have a book.

1. pencil	5. notebook
2. pen	6. marker
3. ruler	7. piece of paper
4. eraser	8. envelope

B. Multiple-slot

The rain in Spain stays mainly on the plain.

1. falls	5. sleet
2. snow	6. France
3. Italy	7. is
4. Switzerland	8. fog

Procedure

1. Instruct the students to substitute the new word in the proper place in the sentence.

2. Model the frame (sentence) and cue. *I have a book. Pencil. I have a pencil.*

3. Say the frame and the cue. *I have a book. Pencil.*

4. The students respond with the substitution. *I have a pencil.*

5. Give the correct response and a new cue. *I have a pencil. Pen.*

6. The students respond. *I have a pen.*

Variations

1. The teacher, after giving the model, gives only the single word substitution.

Teacher says:	Students respond:
Pencil	*I have a pencil.*
Pen	*I have a pen.*

2. Vary the drill from choral responses (everyone responds at once) to individual responses.

Teacher says:	The class responds:
I have a book. Pencil.	*I have a pencil.*
Carlos, I have a pencil. Pen.	Carlos responds: *I have a pen.*

3. Have the class echo the response in unison.

Teacher:	Student:	The class:
I have a book. Pencil.	*I have a pencil.*	*I have a pencil.*

4. Have the students conduct the practice in pairs.

Student:	Other student:
I have a book. Pencil.	*I have a pencil.*

5. Use actual objects or flash cards with pictures of the single word.

Teacher:	Student(s):
I have a book.	
(Holds up picture of) pencil	*I have a pencil.*

6. Write single words on the board and point to them for substitutions.

Teacher:	Student:
I have a book.	
(Points to word "pencil")	*I have a pencil.*

Tactics

Suggestions and Guidelines for Writing Slot Substitution Practices

1. The basic sentence should not be long. 8-10 words is a good length.

2. About 20 items is a good number. Substitution Practices are fairly easy to do as choral exercises. You can write circular drills so that by the time you come to the last item the sentence has returned to the basic frame you started with. This allows you to keep right on going with the practice if you want to go through it a second or third time.

3. In writing multiple slot practices be very careful that the slots are quite distinct from each other. In other words, two noun slots, such as a subject noun and an object noun, would lead to confusion.

4. Some grammatical points that can be practiced through the use of these practices are:

   ◆ subject-verb agreement (a substitution practice can be a conjugation practice put in the context of a complete sentence).

   ◆ word order – when the same sentence pattern is repeated several times, the word order can be fixed in the student's mind.

   ◆ increasing the students' awareness of parts of speech – when forced to pay attention to features such as noun slots, verb slots, adjective slots, etc., the students can pick up a greater awareness of the parts of speech of the substitution items.

   ◆ gender or noun class agreement – when a noun of a different gender or noun class is substituted in a sentence, other words and concords may have to change to agree with the new word.

   ◆ singular-plural distinctions—alternating singular and plural nouns in the noun slot may force changes in agreement elsewhere in the sentence.

Sentence Expansion Practice

Purpose

To give students the opportunity to make more complex sentences. This technique is especially useful for helping them learn how to add modifying words, phrases, and clauses.

Brief Description

The teacher provides a set of instructions that tell the students to add a new element to a basic sentence and make all the necessary changes that the new element will cause. The teacher then gives the basic sentence and a student gives the response. An optional step (shown as part of the procedure) is to have the entire class echo the correct answer, thus giving everyone the opportunity to speak.

Sample Sentence Expansion Practice

Add the word "always" to these sentences.

Mrs. Jackson is busy. > Mrs. Jackson is <u>always</u> busy.

1. John is here.	9. Shirley is in the library.
2. He drinks coffee.	10. I am tired.
3. Steve and Tim are late.	11. He reads *The New York Times*.
4. Fire engines are red.	12. They work on Saturday.
5. The weather here is beautiful.	13. London is foggy.
6. She smokes a pipe.	14. It rains in Calcutta.
7. We drive to work.	15. She answers the phone.
8. Susan types well.	16. They watch television.

Notes

1. Simple expansion drills (like the sample, above) work well with choral responses, but more complicated expansions are better done with individual responses.

2. In the sample, there is very little semantic connection from one basic sentence to the next. This is because the point of the drill is to focus the student's attention on a grammatical feature rather than involve the student in a communicative exchange of information.

Sentence Expansion Exercise

Procedure

1. **Give the instructions.** Add the word *"always"* to these sentences.

2. **Model an example.** *Mrs. Jackson is busy. Mrs. Jackson is always busy.*

3. **Say a sentence.** *John is here.*

4. **The students respond.** *John is always here.*

5. **The class echoes the answer.** *John is always here.*

Variations

1. Change the kinds of student responses, alternating between choral responses, where everyone answers at the same time, and individual responses.

2. To correct a mistake, don't give the correct version to the student. Simply signal that the response is incorrect and allow the student the opportunity to correct it.

3. Two or three different items can be used for expanding the sentence. You can put the items on the board and point to the element to be added to the sentence. Flash cards and oral cues can also be used.

   Put on the board: *never   always   usually   frequently*

   Say: *John is here.* (point to "never")

   The student responds: *John is never here.*

4. The opposite of an expansion practice is a sentence reduction practice. The procedure for doing a reduction practice would be basically the same as the expansion practice. A reduction practice would require the learners to reduce one part of a sentence to a shorter form. Typically, this would involve teaching pronouns, contractions, and other words that represent longer expressions. See Suggestions and Guidelines for samples.

Suggestions and Guidelines for Writing Expansion Practices

1. 12-20 sentences is a good length.

2. Choose vocabulary which is familiar to the students. Stopping to explain new words interferes with the point of the activity – working on grammar.

3. Notice in the sample format that the student is forced to choose where to insert the new element. In sentences 1, 3, 4, 5, 9, 10, and 13, the new element is inserted after the verb, while in the other sentences the new element is inserted before the verb. The point here is that the activity is constructed so that the students have to stay on their toes and consider each response carefully. In other words, mindless repetition or substitution will not be a very successful tactic.

4. Although the sentences in expansion (and reduction) practices in most textbooks are not connected to each other in meaning, if you are writing your own practices, it would be a good idea to have some kind of thematic unity to the sentences. For example, all the sentences could deal with a general theme such as "shopping" or "traveling." An occasional humorous or unusual sentence can add life to the activity.

5. Expansion practices can be used to:

   - add a frequency word (*always, never, often*, etc.)
   - add adjectives (*big, small, long*, etc.)
   - add prepositional phrases (*at the bank, in this room*, etc.)
   - add time phrases (*in the morning, today*, etc.)
   - add a new construction (*Do you know that...*)

Suggestions and Guidelines for Writing Reduction Practices

1. Some points that can be practiced are:

   a. noun   >   pronoun
   (*John   >   he*)

   b. Full form   >   contracted form
   (*I do not have   >   I don't have*)

   c. locative phrases >   locative adverbs
   (*in this room   >   here*)

2. In practicing contracted forms, it may be best to concentrate on having the learners <u>understand</u> rather than speak the contraction, especially when practicing colloquial forms such as "gonna" for "going to." If so, it may be better to present the contracted (reduced) form and have the students respond with the full form.

Sentence Transformation Practice

Purpose

To give students practice in producing major sentence types. Attention is focused on the structural relationships between sentence types, and the changes (transformations) that are necessary to convert one type of sentence to another.

Brief Description

The students are given a sentence with instructions to change the sentence in a particular way – for example, from affirmative to negative, or statement to question, or one verb tense to another.

Sample Sentence Transformation Practice

> **Make the following sentences negative:**
>
> 1. I like pears.
> 2. He wants a camera.
> 3. They understand Spanish.
> 4. You need a haircut.
> 5. I have a dictionary.
> 6. She owns a camera.
> 7. They know all the answers.
> 8. He has a lot of money.
> 9. Marta speaks Spanish.
> 10. We need a dictionary.
> 11. They have my camera.
> 12. She wants to go.
> 13. I know the answer.
> 14. He likes to study Spanish.
> 15. They want more money.
> 16. You have my dictionary.

Sentence Transformation Exercise

Procedure

1. Explain the activity and give the instructions.

2. Model an example.

3. Say a sentence.

4. The students change it.

5;6.   Present another sentence and have the students respond, and so on.

Variations

1. The class can respond in unison, rather than as individuals.

2. After an individual gives an answer, you can ask the whole class to "echo" the student's answer in unison.

3. After the first student changes the sentence into its new form, have the second one change it back to the original.

T:	*He wants a camera.*
S1:	*He doesn't want a camera.*
S2:	*He wants a camera.*

4. Students can do the activity in pairs. One student reads the basic sentence and a second one changes it.

Suggestions and Guidelines for Writing Sentence Transformation Practices

1. Some typical kinds of transformations are:

Statement   >   Question

Affirmative   >   Negative

Affirmative question   >   Negative question

Active   >   Passive

One tense   >   Another tense

Singular subject   >   Plural subject

Formal commands   >   Informal commands

2. About 15-20 sentences should be sufficient for the practice. When dealing with a particular transformation for the first time, keep the sentences short and simple.

3. Because the focus is on grammar, restrict the vocabulary of the sentences to words the students should know. It is best to keep all the basic sentences in the same tense, unless changing the tense is the point of the drill.

Notes:

1. See the Grid Practice (page 101) for a more complex transformation drill.

2. The vocabulary in the sample is purposely limited to common words so that it doesn't get in the way of practicing the transformations. One way to limit the vocabulary is to use the same words several times, as in the sample.

3. As verbs are typically complex word forms, see page 149 for a list of high frequency verbs in English. High frequency verbs in other languages will usually be similar to these English verbs.

Grid Practice

Purpose

To review various sentence types and verb tenses. The grid can be used as a cumulative review exercise, repeating the exercise and expanding on it as a new form is introduced.

Brief Description

The students look at their grid while you give them a cue. They respond with a sentence that fits your cue. There are four possible kinds of cues.

Verb: *go, see, like,* etc.

Person: *John, we, they,* etc.

Type: affirmative, negative, question, imperative, subjunctive, etc.

Tense: *today, yesterday, tomorrow,* etc.

Sample Grid

	AFFIRMATIVE +	NEGATIVE −	QUESTION ?
Every day			
Today			
Yesterday			
Tomorrow			

Procedure

1. Explain the nature of the activity.

2. Model an example or two, giving the cues and a sample response.

3; 4. Give the cue and have the students respond with a sentence (*John didn't go there.*).

5; 6. Continue giving cues while the students add content of their own.

Variations

1. The cues and instructions can be varied in a number of ways. Try several combinations.
2. Make a larger grid for the wall and point to the cues rather than speaking them.
3. Try the exercise occasionally as a rapid-fire game/quiz.
4. Have the students write the responses to the cue.
5. A student can lead the class.
6. Pairs can drill each other.

Notes

1. It is a good idea to develop a series of symbols such as these:

   +   =   affirmative

   −   =   negative sentence

   ?   =   question

   wh   =   question-word sentence

   , ?   =   tag question

2. The tense expression can also be developed into one word or short phrases such as:

   yesterday   =   past tense

   have just   =   present perfect tense

   tomorrow at two o'clock   =   future continuous

3. Warning: there will probably be places where the grid will not work. For example, imperative forms do not fit easily into the grid. Obviously the grid should not be used for forms that will cause confusion.

4. The students have the opportunity to put in some sentence elements of their own. In the sample, one student responded with "*there*" and the second student chose to respond with "*Boston.*"

Tactics Teaching Languages for Communication and Accuracy ◆ **103**

Suggestions and Guidelines for Writing a Grid Practice

1. Although the grid will have to be adapted to fit the language, the sample below for English should provide some ideas.

	+	-	?	-?	+,?	-,+?
every day (simple present)						
now (present progressive)						
yesterday (past)						
going to (future)						
will (future)						
have just (present perfect)						
all week (pres. perf. progr.)						
yesterday at 2:00 (past progr.)						
going to/yesterday (going to - past)						
used to (past habitual)						
should, etc. (modal simple)						
should have, etc. (modal past)						

Key
+ affirmative statement
- negative statement
? question
-? negative question
+,? negative tag question
-,+? affirmative tag question

Chart Pattern Practice

Purpose

To practice a sentence pattern through repetitions of the pattern. The sentences are constructed by the students from visual cues.

Brief Description

A chart containing a series of pictures is used as the basis for practicing a particular sentence pattern or grammatical structure. Usually the pictures are set up in a series so that the students can proceed from one picture to the next without cues from the teacher.

Sample Chart

Yesterday Jim got up at seven o'clock.

Chart Pattern Practice

Procedure

Before starting the practice check that the students are familiar with the vocabulary in the chart.

1. Give the students instructions on what they are supposed to do. In the sample, the students are asked to produce simple past tense. They are also asked to take turns.

2. Model an example.

3. Point at one part of the chart to initiate the practice.

4. The students respond, taking turns.

Variations

1. Use a question and answer chain rather than just one sentence.

    T: *What time did Jim get up yesterday?*
    S1: *He got up at seven o'clock.*
    T: *What time did he take a shower?*
    S2: *He took a shower at 7:15.*
    etc.

2. After completing the chart, ask questions about the pictures in random order.

3. The same chart can be used to practice several different patterns. Each time a new pattern is practiced, previous patterns can be reviewed.

4. Have each student recite all the sentences.

5. Have the students give a personal variation on the original to practice *"I/you"* patterns. In other words, a student might say: *"Yesterday I got up at 8:00."*

Suggestions and Guidelines for Writing Chart Pattern Practices

1. It's easy to make your own stick-figure charts. A good chart needs only 6-10 frames. Some themes for the charts are:

    - ◆ daily routine
    - ◆ weekend routine
    - ◆ school-day routine
    - ◆ a trip to someplace

    - ◆ specific job routines
    - ◆ going to a movie
    - ◆ performing a specific task

2. Sequences (see p. 37) can be good sources for chart practices. For example, a sequence showing a typical baseball action:

    (the pitcher) *holding, throwing,* (the batter) *swinging, hitting, running*
    (the fielder) *catching, throwing,* (the umpire) *signaling safe/out.*

3. Some patterns that can be practiced are:

    Everyday/Yesterday/Tomorrow, Jim . . . (tenses)
    While/Before/When . . . , Jim . . . (adverbial time clauses)
    Jim . . . but . . . (negation)
    Jim . . . After that/Then/Next, . . . (discourse connectors)

3. The charts do not have to have a time sequence. A series of objects can be pictured to practice statements of preference, ability, or comparison. Possible objects: fruit, vegetables, vehicles, furniture, appliances, tools, animals.

    Newspaper circulars, supermarket flyers, and catalogs are possible sources of accessible and inexpensive pictures.

4. Activities or objects in a selected place are another possible source for a chart practice.

 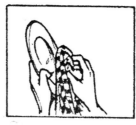  

Illustration from Pat Moran's *Lexicarry*, Pro Lingua Associates

Chart Pattern Practice

Utterance-Response Practice

Purpose

To have the students repeat a sentence pattern or a special expression several times. By changing part of the utterance, you can make the repetition less tiresome. Idioms and formulaic speech can also be practiced in the context of this activity.

Brief Description

This practice is like a two-line dialogue where the teacher makes the utterance and the student responds. The student is expected to respond with a particular sentence pattern.

Sample Utterance Response Practice

Respond to the questions with the following pattern:

Sure, I'd love to. _____ is great fun.

For example:

How would you like to play tennis?

Sure, I'd love to. Playing tennis is great fun.

1. How would you like to dance the cha-cha-cha?
2. How would you like to go to the movies?
3. How would you like to sing folk songs?
4. How would you like to sing karaoke with me?
5. How would you like to take a walk?
6. How would you like to go fishing?
7. How would you like to read poetry?
8. How would you like to listen to folk songs?
9. How would you like to play the guitar?
10. How would you like to look at some photos?
11. How would you like to visit Uncle Paul?
12. How would you like to study grammar?

Other possible exchanges

I prefer (action films, etc.). Me, too. I really like _____./ Oh, I hate them. I prefer ____.

I think I'll have (vanilla, etc.). I will too. I really like _____. / Not me! I'll have _____.

I don't like _____. Me neither./ Really? I really like _____.

Can you _____? Sure, I'd be glad to _____. /Sorry, I'd like to but I can't _____.

Do you have _____? Of course, do you need _____?/ I'm really sorry, but I don't.

Tactics

Utterance-Response Practice

Procedure

1. Explain the purpose and nature of the activity to the students.

2. Model the complete pattern that is to be practiced.

3. Say the utterance.

4. The students respond chorally.

5; 6. The practice continues, and the students take turns responding.

Variations

1. In pairs, the students can make the utterance, as well as the response.

2. You can have two possible responses, and the student can choose one.

   Sure, I'd love to . _____ *is great fun.*
   OR
   Yuck! _____ *is boring.*

3. You can have a three-part utterance, with the third student taking the opposite response.

   T: *How would you like to go skiing?*
   S1: *Sure, I'd love to. Skiing is great fun.*
   S2: *Yuck! Skiing is boring.*

   S2 can then pose the utterance to S3, and so on, in chain fashion.

4. Provide a list of expressions and let the students each choose one. Be careful with intonation and appropriateness, especially with negative responses.

Sure, I'd love to.	*No thanks.*
Right on!	*No way!*
Yes, of course.	*Are you serious?*
Great idea!	*Are you kidding?*
Now you're talking!	*Sorry, that's not for me.*
Why not?	*Not interested.*
Absolutely!	*I don't think so.*

Suggestions and Guidelines for Writing an Utterance-Response Practice

1. This activity can teach both a grammatical feature and idiomatic expressions. The idiomatic expressions could be omitted, but the practice would become much less interesting. In fact, this kind of practice may be more effective for teaching idioms than it is for teaching grammar.

2. Write two-line exchanges that will also be useful for teaching intonation. Have the learners say the sentences dramatically. For example:

   A: *Mario finally passed chemistry.*
   B: *At last! I didn't think he'd ever pass!*

3. Not all utterances and responses are question-answer. Some can be statement-statement, and some can be statement-question. For example:

   Statement: *Mario will never pass chemistry.*
   Statement: *Not a chance! He's terrible at chemistry.*

   Statement: *Mario will never pass chemistry.*
   Question: *Why in the world is he so bad at chemistry?*

Note

This tactic is based on *Utterance-Response Drills* by Jason B. Alter, Roy W. Collier, and Miho Tanaka Steinberg (now out of print, but available on some websites).

Scrambled Sentences

Purpose

This activity is useful for reviewing word order and the placement of punctuation marks. It is also a good way to encourage students to work together as part of a team. While trying to find the solution, the learners are also using the target language for authentic communication (but beware of the use of native languages in monolingual classes). This activity can also be a competitive game to see which person/team finishes all the sentences first.

Brief Description

The students arrange a number of jumbled words and punctuation marks to create sentences. The words may be written on separate index cards, one word and one punctuation mark on each card, and laid out where students can easily move the cards around in front of them. The words may also be presented in electronic form and manipulated by "drag and drop" on a computer or website.

The game or activity may be more effective if it concentrates on a single sentence pattern, e.g., questions in the simple present tense.

Preparation Using Index Cards

1. Write out a sentence with each word on a separate card. An easy activity is to capitalize the first word in the sentence. Punctuation marks can also be included on separate cards. A more challenging version is to write all the words in upper case with no punctuation marks.

2. To prevent mixing up various sentences, number the sentences and then mark each card in a sentence with the same number.

I	THINK	LEARNING	LANGUAGES	IS	FUN
1	1	1	1	1	1

I	WANT	TO	SPEAK	MANY	LANGUAGES
2	2	2	2	2	2

3. Shuffle the cards in each sentence and secure with a rubber band.

4. Keep a list of all the sentences for your own reference. It can also serve as a handout with the answers.

A Sample Game

This sample ESL game features four types of adverbial clauses (causal, conditional, temporal, and concessive).

Let's have a picnic!

Before we leave, let's check the weather report.

Because it may rain, Dan won't go.

Since Dan won't go, let's invite Nancy.

If it's going to rain, shall we stay home?

If we stay home, let's play video games.

In case it rains, let's take an umbrella.

Although it rained, we had a good time.

Because it was cloudy, Michael went home.

While we set the tables, Teddy cooked the hot dogs.

Whenever Teddy cooks, he burns everything.

Even though the hot dogs were burned, we ate them.

After we ate, we went swimming.

While we were swimming, Leslie took a walk.

As she was walking along the trail, she saw an animal.

As it was a very large bear, Leslie ran.

Procedure

1. Divide the class into groups of two or three students.

2. Give each group a sentence and put the extras in the middle of the room.

3. Tell each group that it must use all the cards to form a sentence.

4. When a group is satisfied with its sentence, it writes the number of the sentence and the sentence on a separate sheet of paper (or on the computer or other electronic device). Then the group returns its sentence to the middle and chooses a new bundle of cards.

5. When the groups have finished, read the correct sentences and have the groups check their answers.

Variations

1. Have the groups read their answer sheets to each other.

2. Ask the students if any of the words can be switched around or moved. (e.g., *Sometimes I do my laundry on the weekend. I sometimes do my laundry on the weekend.*)

3. The first group to finish can write its answers on the board or on the computer to project on the board.

4. Instead of working at the sentence level, the learners can try working at the paragraph level, arranging sentences into coherent paragraphs.

5. Instead of concentrating on sentences of the same structure, you may want to use sentences from a short dialogue. After the learners assemble the individual sentences, they would then assemble the most logical order in the dialogue.

Suggestions and Guidelines for Writing Scrambled Sentences

1. The sentences can focus on particular structures, such as questions in the past tense.
2. The sentences can be part of a dialogue that students have read and will be asked to perform.
3. Instead of index cards, smaller pieces about the size of business cards can be used and stored in envelopes.
4. The words can also be written on large pieces of card stock (old file folders) and played as a Line Up (page 21), with each learner holding a card and trying to move into the right order in the line.
5. If there is limited space for laying cards out on the floor or desktops, you can affix magnetic tape to the back of index cards. The cards can be moved around easily on the board.

Note

Short stories such as *Aesop's Fables* and folktales are a nice source of sentences that can be put into a paragraph/discourse order.

Sample Scrambled Paragraph

Tactics

The hare loved to tease the tortoise about its slowness.
In a little while, the hare fell asleep under the tree.
The race began!!
It was almost dark!
Time passed, and the hare woke up.
One day, the tortoise challenged the hare to a race.
There was the tortoise, waiting and smiling.
The hare thought this was very funny,
The hare raced to the finish line,
Immediately, the hare raced far ahead of the tortoise.
but it agreed.
The hare decided to rest under a tree
but it was too late!
and let the tortoise catch up.

The Solution

The hare loved to tease the tortoise about its slowness.
One day, the tortoise challenged the hare to a race.
The hare thought this was very funny,
but it agreed.
The race began!!
Immediately, the hare raced far ahead of the tortoise.
The hare decided to rest under a tree
and let the tortoise catch up.
In a little while, the hare fell asleep under the tree.
Time passed, and the hare woke up.
It was almost dark!
The hare raced to the finish line,
but it was too late!
There was the tortoise, waiting and smiling.

Notes

1. In this sample, the first line is given, to set the scene and give the students a head start.

2. There are three sentences with coordinate or subordinate clauses. This makes the lines shorter, but adds to the challenge – the students have to watch the punctuation.

3. The challenge can be increased even more by also scrambling the sentences and clauses.

Scramble Sentences

Visual Question-Answer Practice

Purpose

To use visual information (pictures) as a basis for developing vocabulary and practicing questions and answers and/or specific grammatical constructions.

Brief Description

An illustration containing several related items is the basis for this practice. The teacher introduces a question-answer exchange and then has the students carry on with the exchange.

Sample Format

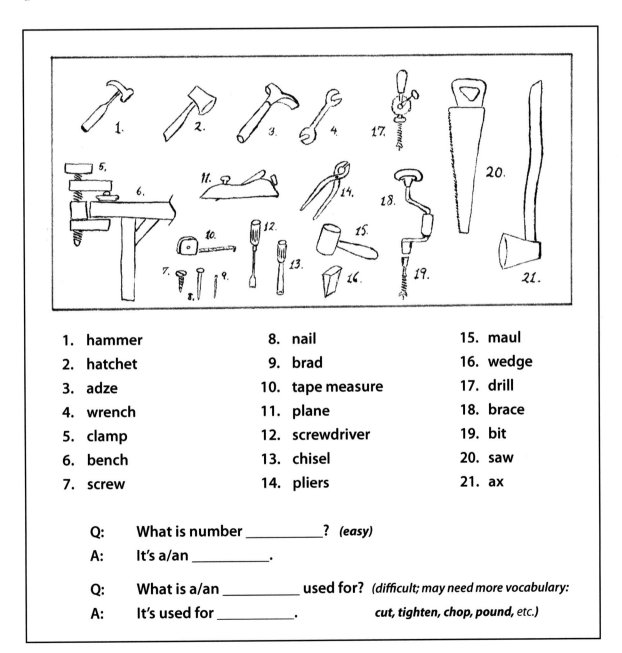

1. hammer	8. nail	15. maul
2. hatchet	9. brad	16. wedge
3. adze	10. tape measure	17. drill
4. wrench	11. plane	18. brace
5. clamp	12. screwdriver	19. bit
6. bench	13. chisel	20. saw
7. screw	14. pliers	21. ax

Q: What is number _____? *(easy)*
A: It's a/an _____.

Q: What is a/an _____ used for? *(difficult; may need more vocabulary:*
A: It's used for _____.   *cut, tighten, chop, pound, etc.)*

Visual Question-Answer Practice

Procedure

1. Explain the nature of the activity (vocabulary development) and how it will be done.

2. Introduce the items and the question-answer pattern. Have the students repeat the name of each item.

3; 4. Begin the practice by asking questions as the students respond. The response can be choral and/or individual.

5. Have the students work in pairs. If possible, have a large illustration or a projected illustration without the words.

Variations

1. This practice can be done as a "chain" practice. For example:

   | 1st Student: | Asks questions. |
   | 2nd Student: | Answers. |

   | 2nd Student: | Asks questions. |
   | 3rd Student: | Answers. |

3rd Student:	Asks questions.
4th Student:	Answers.
etc.	

2. Use the picture without the key list of words and have the students write down the key words as they are dictated.

3. After practicing the patterns for a while, cover up the key words list and have the students try to remember the key words.

4. In the variations above, you could also have the students use rituals such as "Please say that again," or "Would you spell that for me?"

Notes

1. This practice makes no attempt to be conversational or simulate conversational exchanges. The patterns to be practiced are selected for their grammatical and lexical content rather than their communicative potential.

2. This practice can also be very useful for teaching technical or specialized vocabulary.

Tactics

Suggestions and Guidelines for Writing Visual Question-Answer Practices

1. A good format is two questions with their corresponding answers, although more advanced classes can probably handle at least one more question-answer pair.

2. Twenty items is a comfortable number of items to work with.

3. Picture dictionaries are an excellent source for illustrations. Oxford, Cambridge, Longmans (Pearson), Cengage, and others all publish ESL picture dictionaries. Pro Lingua's *Lexicarry* does not have the words on the page with the pictures. Thus, it can be used with any language.

4. A wide variety of grammatical constructions can be practiced through the use of this technique. Some possible questions that could be asked about the sample illustration are:

   Do you have/own a _____?

   Have you ever used a _____?

   Why would you use a_____?

   Which tool is better for _____?

   How much do you think a _____ costs?

   If I want to _____ what should I use?

5. You can play a guessing game. A student chooses an object, and the other students try to find out what they are by asking questions, such as, "Are you big? Can I hold you? Are you metal?"

6. Other possible visuals:

   fruit, vegetables, vehicles, rooms in a house, office equipment, classroom supplies, street scene, clothing, appliances, sporting equipment, boats, animals, personal paraphernalia (comb, key, coin, etc.), professions/occupations

Spontaneous Pattern Practice

Purpose

To practice a sentence pattern that uses information created by the student. The personal involvement on the student's part makes the practice much more interesting and memorable.

Brief Description

The teacher gives a model sentence that contains some blanks. The teacher inserts personal information in the blank, and then through a series of questions, has each student create a sentence of their own. The student's own sentence then becomes the basis for further questions and answers.

Sample Formats

If I had a thousand dollars, I would _____.

My favorite weekend activity is _____.

When I order a pizza, I ask for _____.

I have never been to (Paris, etc.).

(Madrid, etc.) is the world's greatest city.

My next car is going to be _____, because _____.

My favorite (school) subject is _____ ,
    and my least favorite is _____ .

My father is/was a _____,
    and my mother is/was _____.

Spontaneous Pattern Practice

Procedure

1. Explain the purpose and nature of the activity and what the students will do.

2. Model the basic pattern and supply your own information.

3; 4. Ask the students to follow the model with their own information.

5;6. Ask the students to respond with a classmate's information.

Variations

1. The teacher asks each student about the other students' sentences.

2. Have the students ask "you" questions (S5, what would you do?).

3. Have each student ask "he/she" questions (S5, what would S2 do?).

4. Have each student ask "who" questions (Who would go to California?).

5. Have each student tell what all the other students would do.

6. Have the students write all the sentences they have created.

Notes

1. The students may make mistakes as they create a sentence. The teacher should correct the sentences. One way to correct is to ask a question, emphasizing the incorrect part. For example:

    S: *I would go to the California.*
    T: *You would go to THE California?*

2. Keep the practice limited to one sentence per student.

3. Have the students keep a notebook of these practices. It will help personalize their language course.

Suggestions and Guidelines for Writing a Spontaneous Pattern Practice

This practice is good for working on verb phrases, especially complicated phrases.

Some samples are:

Yesterday I _____.

Tomorrow I'm going to _____.

Last year at this time I was _____.

If I had _____, I would _____.

Yesterday I was going to _____, but _____.

_____ isn't in class; he might be _____.

Last night I was _____ when _____.

Instead of _____, I wish I could _____.

Whenever I _____, I _____.

Yesterday I wanted to _____, but I couldn't because I had to _____.

I really ought to _____, but I would rather _____.

Question Word Analysis

Purpose

To give the students practice in comprehending a sentence using question words. Secondarily, the students will increase their awareness of the phrase structure of a sentence and will increase their ability to respond to and use the basic question words (*what, who, when, where, why, how*).

Brief Description

The teacher reads a sentence and then asks question-word questions about it. The students respond with short answers. Each short answer is part of the sentence. All the short answers together form the entire sentence. This practice takes the sentence apart and (optionally) puts it back together again.

Sample Format

Listen to the sentence and answer the questions with short answers.

1. John is walking to the library.
   a. Who is walking to the library?
   b. What is he doing?
   c. Where is he walking to?

2. He usually studies in the library for two hours.
   a. Who studies in the library?
   b. Where does he study?
   c. How long does he study?
   d. How often does he study in the library?

3. John doesn't go to the library on Saturdays.
   a. When doesn't he go to the library?
   b. Where doesn't he go on Saturdays?
   c. Who doesn't go to the library on Saturdays?

4. Yesterday he wrote a term paper on art for Professor Smith.
   a. What kind of paper did he write?
   b. What was the paper on?
   c. Who did he write it for?
   d. What did he do?
   e. When did he do it?

Question Word Analysis

Procedure

1. Explain the activity.

2. Model an example, giving the sentence, the question, and the answer.

3; 4. Ask the students questions and have them answer with short answers. (If they respond with the full sentence, you can't be sure they have recognized the question word.)

5. Finally, have the students say the whole sentence.

Variations

1. After the questioning, ask a student to recite the entire sentence.

2. Read the sentence and have one of the students pose the questions to a second student, who answers and then questions the third student in chain fashion.

3. Emphasize one part as you read the sentence and have the students form the question for the emphasized part. For example:

   T: *John is <u>walking</u> to the library.*
   S: *What is John doing?*

4. *"Yes/No"* and *"either/or"* questions can also be used.

Notes

1. This technique can be useful for teaching long sentences which are difficult to reproduce from memory after having heard them only once.

2. The sentences can form part of a longer passage.

3. It is not a good idea for the students to respond to the questions with full sentences (except as the final step). Fragments are better because they indicate that the student has in fact understood the question.

4. Default word order in an English sentence can be demonstrated by question words.

   Who/What – Did What – To What/Whom – How – Where –
   When/What time – How Often – What for/Why

Suggestions and Guidelines for Writing a Question-Word Analysis

1. Virtually any sentence in the language can be subjected to a question-word analysis. Therefore, model sentences are everywhere, although descriptive sentences are probably the best type. Sentences from a dialogue are somewhat more difficult to use than sentences from a prose passage.

2. Some key question words and phrases are:

Things	*What*
	Which
	What kind
People	*Who*
	Whose
	Whom
Manner	*How*
Place	*Where*
Direction	*To/From where*
Time	*When*
	How long
Frequency	*How often*
Purpose	*What for*
Reason	*Why/ How come*
Size	*How large*
Distance	*How far*
Qualities	*What color*
Quantity	*How many*

Action Chain

Purpose

To practice grammatical structures in the context of simple actions associated with sentences.

Brief Description

The students and teacher carry out a series of actions, interacting and talking about the actions. The series of sentences that accompany the action usually follow the sequence of command, question, and answer.

Sample Action Chain

_____, look at _____.

What are you doing ?
I'm looking at _____.

Say <u>(hello)</u> to _____.
<u>(Hello).</u>

What did you do?
I said hello to _____.

Ask her how she is doing.
_____, how are you (doing)?
I'm fine, thanks.

What did she say?
She said _____.

Now ask to borrow her book.
_____, may I borrow your book ?

What did she say ?
She said _____.

Procedure

1. After explaining the nature of the activity, initiate the chain with a command.

2. Have a student respond with the appropriate action.

3. Ask the student a question about the action.

4. The students respond as they are performing the action.

5; 6. Continue with a new commands and responses.

7. You can also change the tense of the question.

Variations

1. Ask a third student "he/she" questions.

> **T**: *S1, look at S2.*
> **T**: *S3, what is S1 doing?*
> **S3**: *He's looking at S2.*

2. Have a student give the commands and ask the questions.

3. Have two people perform the chain and ask "you (plural)/we" questions.

4. Have two people perform the actions and ask "they" questions.

5. Have the students work together in pairs or small groups.

6. Simon Says is another possibility, but instead of using "Simon says" as the cue, use "Please."

7. As with sequences, you can practice a variety of tenses within one chain.

Notes

1. This technique is useful for practicing several pronoun forms.

2. These actions must be done deliberately so that the students' verbal and physical responses are coordinated. It can be confusing to say "What are you doing" when the action has been completed and the correct response would be in the past tense.

3. This is a good technique for both introducing and practicing action verbs.

Tactics

Suggestions and Guidelines for Writing an Action Chain

1. Some classroom activities could be:

    ◆ giving and taking something
    ◆ writing and erasing on the board
    ◆ standing and sitting
    ◆ dropping and picking up a pencil, book, etc.
    ◆ speaking, mumbling, singing, humming
    ◆ opening and closing doors and windows
    ◆ turning the lights on and off

2. A sequence for practicing the future tense is:

    T: *S1, please _____ . Wait!*
    What are you going to do?
    S1: *I'm going to _____ .*

3. A possible long sequence could be:

    ◆ command: *Stand up!*
    ◆ past tense question: *What did you do?*
    ◆ past tense answer: *I stood up.*
    ◆ command: *Sit down! Wait!*
    ◆ future tense question: *What are you going to do?*
    ◆ future tense answer: *I'm going to sit down.*
    ◆ present tense question: *What are you doing right now?*
    ◆ present tense answer: *I'm sitting down.*
    ◆ present perfect question: *What have you just done?*
    ◆ present perfect answer: *I have just stood up and sat down.*

Cumulative Chain Practice

Purpose

To practice grammatical structures in the context of information created by the students.

Brief Description

The teacher initiates the chain with a piece of information, typically something they like or dislike or even both. The students, as in a line-up, repeat what the teacher said, and add their own information. This continues as each student repeats what has been said previously.

Sample Cumulative Chain Practice

T: Let's talk about vegetables that we don't like.

T: I really don't like beets.

S1: The teacher doesn't like beets, and I don't like kale.

S2: The teacher doesn't like beets, Raoul doesn't like kale, and I don't like garlic.

S3: The teacher doesn't like beets, Raoul doesn't like kale, Farah doesn't like garlic, and I don't like spinach.

S4: The teacher doesn't like beets, Raoul doesn't like kale, Farah doesn't like garlic. Li doesn't like spinach, and I don't like cabbage.

S5: Etc.

Cumulative Chain Practice

Procedure

1. Set up the situation (e.g., vegetable dislikes and/or likes)

2. Model the basic sentence with your personal item.

3. Point to the first student and have them give their answer.

4. Show them the cumulative pattern : The teacher _____, and I _____.

5. Demonstrate with the second student, whose sentence becomes:
   The teacher _____, S1 _____, and I _____.

6. Continue building the chain.

Variations

1. Have two teams line up and compete to see who can successfully get to the end of the line and complete the chain first.

2. The teacher as initiator can also be the last one.

3. When the chain is completed the students can quiz the teacher: "Teacher, who doesn't like carrots?"

4. Another kind of cumulative chain can be done without cumulation. For example,

IF chain

T: *If I go to Boston this weekend, I'll go to a baseball game.*
S1: *If the teacher goes to a baseball game, he'll buy a hot dog.*
S2: *If he buys a hot dog, he'll buy a drink.*
S3: *If he buys a drink, he'll spill it.*
S4: *If he spills it, he'll be angry.*
S5: *If he is angry he won't enjoy his hot dog.*
S6: *If he doesn't enjoy his hot dog, he'll get angrier.*
S7: *If he gets angrier he won't enjoy the game.*
S8: *If he doesn't enjoy the game he'll go home.*

Suggestions and Guidelines for Writing a Cumulative Chain Practice

1. Some possible initiators:

   I have been to (country).

   My favorite (book, etc.) is ____.

   If I could (be an animal, etc.) I would ____.

   If I won the lottery, I would ____.

   When I am rich I will buy a (Ferrari, etc).

   When I was six years old, I lived in _____.

2. Some possible likes/dislikes/favorites:

car	drink	city
song	dessert	movie
musical group	book	actor
pastime	academic subject	weekend activity
sport	TV program	housework

Note

At the start of the course, this can be a good way to help students learn each other's names without calling attention to them. Write students' names on the board in order in which they appear going around the room, or distribute a handout with their names and have them fill in the information about who like/dislikes which foods, etc.

For those who need an extra challenge, you can include examples of "Neither does X/ And so does X."

Match It

Purpose

To help students practice vocabulary by focusing on meaning, usage, and pronunciation. Secondly to practice speaking while trying to solve a problem (finding the match).

Brief Description

The students may know this as a game called "Concentration" in which players try to identify two items that make a pair. The goal of the game/practice is to make the most matches. This activity is best played in pairs or teams of three. In the classroom, the items are usually on a set of cards placed face down with numbers on the back. For example, pairs can be from a list of :

◆ Idioms and their meanings: *Make up one's mind/decide*
◆ Phonetic symbols and words containing those sounds: /EE/ **eat; feel;** /I/ *fit;* **build**
◆ Pictures and words: *Socks* *Shoes*
◆ Affixes: **En- + large; mal- + function; re- + play; short + -en**

Sample Match It *(verb and collocation with household items)*

The cards can be prepared like this: A matches B; C matches D; E matches F. But the numbers are marked on the back in random order, so that , "vacuum" has 7 on the back and "carpet" has 19.

A	B	C	D	E	F
Vacuum 7	Carpet 19	Weed 12	Garden 5	Cook 10	Meals 2
Mop 22	Kitchen floor 15	Do 24	Dishes 1	Take out 23	Trash 17
Dust 18	Furniture 4	Set 14	Table 13	Water 8	Plants 20
Mow 11	Lawn 21	Make 6	Bed 9	Feed 16	Cat 3

Note that the cards are set out as below; face down are the sides with the words. Thus, 1, which is *dishes*, would match with 24, "do," and 7 and 19 match as "vacuum" and "carpet."

1	2	3	4	5	6
7 (vacuum)	8	9	10	11	12
13	14	15	16	17	18
19 (carpet)	20	21	22	23	24

Procedure

1. Prepare a set of matches and paste or print onto index cards.

2. Shuffle the cards and then number them on the back.

3. Lay the cards out with numbers face up.

4. The first player calls out the numbers of two cards and then turns them over. If they are a match, the player keeps the pair; if not a match, the cards are turned over again and the next player tries to make a match.

5. The students must use the target language.

6. A list of game-playing expressions on the board, or posted where all can see, may include:

    That's a match!

    Too bad. Tough luck!

    It's your turn.

    That's cheating! You're/He's/She's cheating!

    You won!

Variations

1. Give one point for a match, and another for correct use.
2. If the students need to review the items or pronunciation before playing, begin by laying the cards out in random order and have the class or group match them all face up in two columns, checking to see that the matches are correct.
3. If the class is large or the students are beginners, they may play as teams and may consult with each other to check their memory of which cards might match.

Suggestions and Guidelines for Match It

If making more than one copy of the game, use different colored stock or cards to help keep the copies separate.

Note

Pro Lingua publishes *Match It!*, a book of 83 photocopyable matching games, easy to challenging.

Pictogram

Purpose

This activity requires students to speak clearly, sharpen listening skills, and ask clarifying questions.

Brief Description

The students are paired and seated back-to-back to remove facial clues and other body language. Student A is given something to describe to Student B, who will try to reproduce or identify the item based on A's description. The students compare the results afterwards and then switch roles, with B describing something to A.

Sample Back-to-Back Activities

1. Drawing: Student A: *In the middle of the paper, draw a circle about three inches in diameter. In the middle of the circle draw a triangle.* Student B: Draws as directed and asks questions to clarify. *Is the triangle touching the circle?*

2. Construction with Objects: Student A directs B: *Place two blue* (Cuisenaire) *rods so they are parallel to each other and about two centimeters apart. Lay a red rod on top of two blue ones.*

3. Picture Description: Student A has a picture and describes it to Student B who draws the picture without seeing it. For example, a simple picture with easy vocabulary would be:

Procedure

1. Review the vocabulary and directions needed by giving a short demonstration with a volunteer.

2. Have the students pair off and position themselves so they are back to back, seated on the floor or in chairs. Have them decide who is A and who is B.

3. Provide the students with the materials – colored rods, colored pens, etc.

4. Student A gives directions. B may ask for clarification. When finished, they compare the results and discuss any differences.

Variations

1. The students may repeat the activity with different partners, giving them another opportunity to practice and improve skills.

2. Each pair is given a picture which is similar to the others but somewhat different. The describers are given a time limit to describe their picture. The listeners do not draw; they just listen, but may ask questions. Warn the describer not to show the picture even after the time limit is announced. When the time is up, pick up all the pictures and put them on a table or a whiteboard tray. The listeners look at the pictures and each tries to find the one their partner described. They bring their choice back to the describer for confirmation. The samples on page 141 and 142 may be photocopied.

3. Give student A a sheet of paper such as the sample below. Give student B an envelope containing the same piece of paper cut up -- in the case of the sample, cut into seven different triangles. It is best to have one side of the sheet colored.

4. Try the Online Free software to drag and drop furniture into a classroom outline. http://classroom4teachers.org

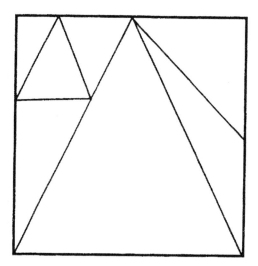

Suggestions and Guidelines for Making Back-to-Back Activities

1. Prepositions will be important in this activity. Therefore it is good to be sure the students have practiced them before doing the activity.

2. Postcards showing similar scenes may be useful. For example: various views of the Golden Gate Bridge (or other bridges), a city skyline, baseball stadiums, beaches, covered bridges, lighthouses.

3. Postage stamps, although small, usually have a limited number of objects depicted on them. There are sets of stamps with similar objects – different fishes, birds, plants, etc.

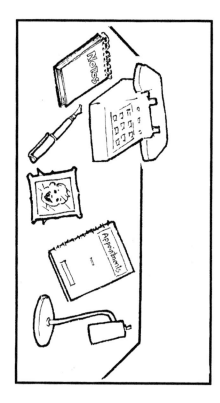

Pictograms

Lexicolor

Purpose

To expand the students' vocabulary by recording, analyzing, and practicing new words as they occur in various sources that the students encounter. Additionally, the students will increase their knowledge and skill in using affixes and recognizing parts of speech.

Brief Description

This activity can be either planned or unplanned. In a planned activity, the students are exposed to a chunk of material that will intentionally have probable unknown vocabulary. As an unplanned activity, new words are encountered unintentionally. In either case, the word is "captured" on poster paper and "explored" for pronunciation, meaning, and usage. Using affixation, wherever possible the word is expanded. For example the word *act* can become *react, enact, activity,* etc. Collocations can also be explored: to depend *on*, commit *a crime.* Compound words can also be explored: *underground.*

Procedure

1. The students encounter a new word, and it is written on a sheet of poster paper in color. This will become a posted wall chart. Usually only content words are "captured."

   Nouns are red

   Verbs are green

   Adjectives are blue

   Adverbs are purple

   Function words and most prefixes are black

3. The class uses the context to work toward the meaning. The teacher guides and leads the class in formal, semantic, and pragmatic expansion, principally through affixation. Prefixes in black. Suffixes in the appropriate color, as above.

5. The wall chart is reviewed on a regular basis.

WEEK OF: 1/14/13

explode green
explosion red
im   sive blue
black
     ly purple

          green   red
occur ence
recur green

destroy green
     uctive blue
     uction red

structure red
infra black   al blue

          green
built green
dependable blue   rebuild green
in   ent blue   black
        ly purple
     ence red
depend on green

finance red
          ial green ly purple

expand green able blue
     se red
     sion red

recover green
dis black able blue
un black
cover up green

Manipulations

Purpose

To give the students the opportunity to practice a limited amount of the language (and hence a limited number of grammatical structures) in a meaningful conversational way.

Brief Description

The focus is on objects which can be brought into the classroom. The teacher sets up a situation which requires the students to manipulate the objects and talk about the objects and the manipulations.

Sample Formats

A. Use the following objects: a book, a pen, a pencil, a notebook.

Questions: Who has a _____?
Who doesn't have a _____?

Answers:

I			
You			
He	don't	has	a
She	doesn't	have	
We			
They			

B. With several different kinds of fruit or vegetables:

A. Raoul, take an orange.
B. Farah, take Raoul's orange.
C. Yukiko, who took Raoul's orange?
D. Farah, give the orange to Omar.
E. Omar what did Farah do?
F. Carmen, take two apples.
G. Throw one to Ahmed.
etc.

Procedure

1. After explaining the activity, set up the manipulables. For the sample Format A, the items are handed out to the learners. With sample Format B, the items can be displayed on a table in the center of the classroom.

2. Ask the students questions such as *"Who has a book?"*

3. The students respond.

4; 5. The practice can continue with a new question.

6. In pairs the students can continue the practice as you observe and take notes.

Variations

1. After introducing the basic pattern, let the students carry on with all the questions and answers. As the teacher, you step aside from the role of class leader to listen and correct. With a large class, have the students work in pairs or trios. With a small class this may not be necessary.

2. Tell the students before you begin that once the basic pattern has been introduced, you will not interrupt with corrections. It will be up to the students to ask for confirmations and corrections if they need to.

3. Have the students seated in a circle facing outward so that they cannot see each other. Give everyone an object and have them find out what everyone is doing with their object by asking and answering questions. Allow only yes/no questions: "Yusuf, are you holding your object?"

4. Collect a box of "things" for props. It is easy to build a large collection of small things such as pencils, tacks, matches, paper clips, rubber bands, stamps, envelopes, etc. You could make thematic collections (office things, natural things such as sticks, stones, seeds, household things, classroom things, etc.)

5. Other "things" for manipulations:

   ◆ dice for practicing numbers
   ◆ dominos for numbers and placements
   ◆ Legos or Tinkertoys for putting things together
   ◆ count and noncount items in small plastic bags (*salt, pepper, sugar, basel, rice, lentils, peas, beans, popcorn, M&Ms*, etc.)
   ◆ plastic Fruit
   ◆ bags of plastic animals can be found in most dollar stores

Note

The Silent Way approach to language teaching uses a bag of multi-colored wooden rods of varying sizes, similar to those used for teaching math to children. These rods have advantages in that they are highly portable, inexpensive, and abstract enough to be used in a wide variety of situations.

Suggestions and Guidelines for Writing Manipulations

1. The objects can be useful for teaching the grammar of the noun phrase. For example:

   a. Gender or noun classes.

   b. Agreement of nouns and adjectives.

   c. Singular and plural forms.

   d. Count and non-count nouns.

   e. Word order of modifying adjectives.

   f. Definite and indefinite articles.

2. Some basic sentences that can be used are:

   a. Questions and answers such as:

   > *Do you have, need, want, like, see, etc.*
   > *Who has, wants, needs, etc.*
   > *What does _____ want, need, like, etc.*

   b. Commands and responses such as:

   > *Give _____ to _____ .*
   > *Take _____ from _____ .*
   > *Lend _____ to _____ .*

   c. Descriptions such as:

   > *I have a large green grammar book.*

   d. Prepositions:

   > *Put the _____ next to/ on top of/ beside/ over/ between, etc., the _____ .*
   > *Where is the _____ ?*

Highest-Frequency English Verbs*

Irregular

be	leave		
begin	lose		
bring	make		
buy	mean		
come	put		
cost	read		
cut	say		
do	see		
drink	sit		
eat	sleep		
forget	speak		
get	take		
give	tell		
go	think		
have	understand		
hear	write		
know			

Regular

answer	stop
close	study
enter	talk
excuse	thank
help	try
learn	turn
listen	use
like	wait
live	walk
need	want
open	watch
pull	
push	
remember	
return	
shop	
spell	

*Based on *The Learner's Lexicon*, R. Clark, Pro Lingua
(The 61 verbs above are in the 0-300 word [survival] level)

Other Pro Lingua Books Useful in Teacher Training

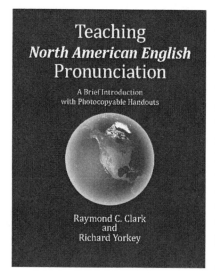

Teaching North American English Pronunciation

This book is for the person who is helping a learner of North American English develop and improve their pronunciation. Part One introduces the basics of English phonology for teacher training with reference to the writing system that represents it. Part Two is a collection of photocopyable handouts that can be used to help English language learners of all ages from the high beginning to advanced proficiency.

For the teacher, using the two parts of the book can be a "Teach as you learn, learn as you teach" professional development experience in a face-to-face classroom context with learners, or the book can be used as a self-study course. The latter learning experience would definitely be enhanced by the use of the CD's.

There is a brief appendix that includes problem areas for different learners of English, and a compilation of phonetic alphabets.

Understanding Teaching Through Learning

can be used as a course book for teacher training courses or teacher development workshops. It also works well as a self-study book used by individuals or small groups.

New and experienced teachers benefit from the thought-provoking exercises and readings.

Creating a learning-centered classroom

Theories and practices of effective classroom language teaching are developed using reflective and analytic tools. Readers explore their own views of language learning and teaching through experiential activities, readings, and exercises resulting in action plans that make sense for their own classrooms. Although many of the examples focus on language learning, the frameworks can easily be applied to other content areas, providing a solid foundation in teaching and learning for instructors of many different subjects.

Pro Lingua also publishes many other resources for language teaching. **Lexicarry** and **Faces** by Patrick Moran are designed to be used teaching any language; Dr. Moran's notes on using these materials are valuable resources for teacher training. Two other books are designed for use with any language: **TalkAbouts** and **Go Fish**. Many other Pro Lingua texts and teacher resources, particularly our many game-playing materials, though written specifically for teaching English language learners, can be adapted for other teaching situations – teaching other languages, reading, or writing, or working with students with learning disabilities. **The ESL Miscellany** is compendium of ideas and materials that are often used in teacher training and in developing materials for many teaching situations.

Information on all of Pro Lingua's publications, often with sample materials that can be reviewed on line or printed for classroom trial, is available at **Pro Lingua Associates. com.**